THE POTATO BOOK

This book is dedicated to my favorite potato in
the world, my beautiful pug Kipper, whom we sadly
lost in March 2024, just before his 10th birthday.

You were beige like a potato. You were comforting
like a potato. You were my best friend and we are
so lucky to have had you in our lives.

THE POTATO BOOK

PHOTOGRAPHY BY ELLIS PARRINDER

POPPY COOKS

101 RECIPES FROM THE POTATO QUEEN

appetite
by RANDOM HOUSE

This Is It

The book that dreams were made of. For all the carb-lovers, potato enthusiasts and spud connoisseurs. This is my all-potato recipe book.

That's right, every single recipe is a spud. Pages on pages of just pure potato. Is this the very reason I was put on this earth? To deliver to you this book of potato bliss? If so, it was a worthwhile life.

I've dreamt of this book for years. Potatoes on potatoes, on potatoes, with a side of potatoes. Every page you turn is just more delicious potato dishes to dig into. Cook your way through it, enjoy every moment, and appreciate the humble spud even more than before.

The question I get asked more than any is, *"When are you making a potato book?"* and, well, the answer is, now. It took a bit longer because I wanted to make this one special. I knew the Potato Queen couldn't let you down, so a lot of blood, sweat and butter went into these pages.

But if you are new here, you might think, what started your love of potatoes?

But if You Are New Here, You Might Think, What Started Your Love of Potatoes?

This is another question that I get asked a lot. Well, I often feel like I resonate a lot with a potato. I'm round. I'm friendly. I'm versatile. I like to be covered in butter. All the usual things.

For me, though, it's the accessibility of the potato that I love so much. It's cheap, it's easy, and everyone can get their hands on it. It means every family can make a potato special in their own home, relatively easily and without too much hassle.

Although I trained in Michelin-starred restaurants, I never wanted to be a chef who just cooked food that rich people could afford. I wanted to make delicious, decadent food that people can make at home – and the potato is the perfect embodiment of that. Spuds can be fancy, but even fancy spuds are achievable in the comfort of your own kitchen.

The potato is also like that friend you can introduce to any other friends and just know they'll get on like a house on fire. And the potato loves all the things that I love: garlic, cheese, butter. All winning combos.

When developing dishes in restaurant kitchens, you're forever thinking about what the carb of the dish is going to be, and potato is often the answer. Potatoes are also a staple. One of the first things you learn in culinary school is how to make the smoothest mashed potatoes. Where would British "bangers and mash" be with only sausages? And what about "fish and chips" without the "chips"? The potato shouldn't just be the accompaniment, it should be the star.

Let's talk about how I became known as the online "Potato Queen", or "that British Potato girl", or even, as coined by Nigella, the "High Priestess of Potatoes". My online love of spuds happened on a bit of a... whim ... coincidentally.

For a start, I never planned to make a career out of making cooking videos. I was working my way up through kitchens, hoping to one day own my own restaurant. I'd worked in Michelin-starred kitchens, experimental fine-dining restaurants, and corporate catering jobs serving rich bankers their lunch. I loved everything about chef-life (other than the 70-hour weeks) and at age 26 had worked up to a Junior Sous Chef in a members' club in Mayfair (the next rank would be Sous Chef, then Head Chef).

It was in March 2020 where a little thing called Covid-19 came about and threw a spanner in the works. I was called into the office one day and told, "The restaurant will be closing for the foreseeable future and we're not sure when we'll be able to open back up, so we're making you redundant." I packed up my stuff from the locker, got on the subway home, cried a bit, then wondered what on earth I was going to do next.

The whole country – the whole world – was in turmoil at the time, so it was hard to feel too sorry for myself as I turned on the daily announcements. But I definitely felt a sense of loss. I'd worked so hard over the years – and particularly in this last role where I had consistently dedicated 70 hours of my life every week to help run a kitchen. 6am mornings. Giving up weekends. Missing parties. Missing funerals. Not seeing my boyfriend and pugs other than getting home at 12:30am to them already snoring away in bed, and leaving again at 6am as they were still all snoring. It felt like I'd dedicated a lot of my life to something that was just suddenly dropped. It felt rubbish.

My partner and I (and the snoring pugs) moved home to my parents for a few months as the country went into lockdown. They lived in the countryside in Worcestershire, so we thought at least we'd be able to go on more nice walks to keep us occupied rather being stuck in the concrete jungle of London.

There's a big age gap between me and my little brother Christian (12 years old at the time I moved home) and sister Trixie (who was 10). They were passing the time scrolling on a new app called TikTok. I'd already downloaded it and had seen it was full of dance videos, lip-syncs and transitions. But at home with my siblings, I began using the app more and I saw some foodie content on there and thought, "You know what? I could do that!" So, I gave it a good go. Please don't scroll back to see those first videos as they were absolutely terrible. I started off with a traditional tomato sauce recipe (I know... no potatoes!). Within a couple of days, someone had commented that they were an essential worker who had been working at the hospital on the night, then made the sauce for the whole family and they loved it. This made me realize that I could actually help people in a tough time, even just a small amount, so I kept going. In some ways I kept posting videos to keep myself busy during lockdown; in other ways it also made me feel cool when my brother and sister were impressed with even 1,000 views on a video, but, mostly, I fell in love with being able to teach people and improve their day in even the slightest way.

Jump to August 2020 and back in London. I think my TikTok platform had grown to about 50,000 followers which felt HUGE. In reality, though, I was still very much unemployed and was actually applying for jobs in local supermarkets, as although it sounded cool to have 50k people following me, it wasn't paying the rent. But, then, I made a famous steak dinner. And it was famous because of one thing – the potatoes. They were crispy. Crispy cube potatoes. Fun fact: I actually didn't film myself making them. At this point, after being rejected from a night shift job at a supermarket, and being six months unemployed, I'd fallen out of love with TikTok and making videos, so probably couldn't be bothered. It was only when my boyfriend ate these crispy cubes of potato-ey goodness and said, "Did you film these? Because they're incredible" that I videoed the end product, then worked backwards and re-did the prep on camera so I could post it. That video went on to be my first to hit 1 million views. Thanks for that, Tom!

When the UK went into a second lockdown for the whole of November, I realized the country would be at home, on their phone, bored, and could do with cheering up. Plus, the crispy cube video had proven exactly what people wanted... spuds. This is where the brainchild of my new series was born: 25 Potatoes Recipes To Get You Through The Second Lockdown. I know, catchy title, right?

During this series, my followers rose to about 250,000 on TikTok, which, again, felt HUGE. I made a compilation video of all the potato recipes I'd just made and put on a posh voice, to say "Hello and welcome to Potato TikTok". It was a short 15-second video, easy to make, nothing special, just shots of delicious potatoes while I spoke in a very British accent saying things like "Live potato, love potato and laugh potato." I went to bed thinking nothing of it. And I woke up to 1 million followers overnight.

This is where potatoes became my life. It turns out, if you post anything other than potatoes after amassing 1 million followers from them, you get quite a lot of comments asking, "Where are the potatoes?" So, I embraced it, and went FULL POTATO in all my content. I'm talking series after series loaded with spuds, from "Around the World in 80 Potatoes" and "A–Z of Potatoes", through my annual "12 Days of Christmas Potatoes" to "Cooking Potatoes Every Single Day until I Physically Implode". I obviously love a short, snappy title.

That's a lot of potatoes. Over 1 billion views-worth of potato videos, actually. Which sounds absolutely mind-blowing. Especially as I remember being that unemployed trying-to-be-cool older sister showing off my 10k video views at one point. I am absolutely blown away by everything I've achieved in the last four years and I can confidently say it was because of potatoes. Over five million followers on my channels, best-selling cookbooks, becoming a regular chef on some of my favorite UK TV shows and appearing as a judge and expert on different cooking competitions, too. Actually, North American Networks, where is my call?!

Potatoes changed my life. And with this book, they can change your life, too.

Is it Normal for Potatoes to Make You Feel a Certain Type of Way?

Yes, Yes it is.

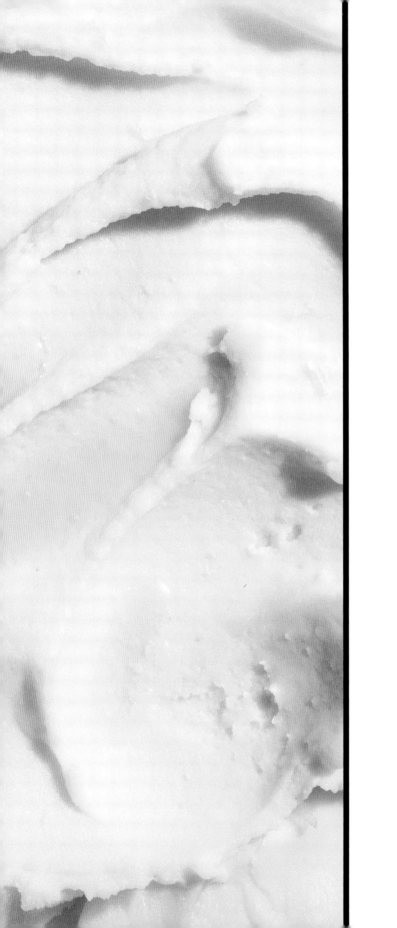

Chapter One

Mashed Potatoes

THE CLASSIC
MASHED POTATOES

1¼ lbs Yukon Gold
  potatoes, peeled

salt, enough to
  make the water
  taste like the sea

5 Tbsp butter, cubed

7 Tbsp heavy cream

Let's talk mashed potatoes, or just "mash" to us Brits – an often-underrated member of the potato family. Forget about that lumpy stuff you ate at school. Mashed potatoes should be creamy, decadent deliciousness. With love, it should blow your socks off. Welcome to my MASHTERCLASS (that's mash-masterclass) in how to achieve the perfect mashed potatoes – a bold claim, I know, but I really believe this is the best way to make the smoothest, creamiest potatoes going.

─────

1. Slice your potatoes into ¾-inch-thick rounds, which cooks them more evenly. Place the potatoes in a saucepan and just cover with cold water – you want a pan that fits all the potato rounds without them overlapping too much. If you pile all the potatoes on top of each other, the bottom spuds will cook quicker than the ones on top. Use a pan that is deep and wide enough that the potatoes fit almost in a single layer. It doesn't have to be exact, but I promise you – getting this right will make your mash SMOOTH.

2. Add a massively generous amount of salt – like I said over in the ingredients, the water should taste like the sea. The reason for this is osmosis, which makes food taste better and helps it hold in more nutrients. Get those potatoes on the heat and let them simmer – not boil. This will also help them to evenly cook.

3. The spuds should cook for around 20 minutes, but test that they are ready by poking a knife into a few of them. If they slide straight off, we are good to go. Drain them in a colander.

4. If you've ever made one of my potato recipes before, you'll know I'm a big fan of a steam-dry, but in case you are one of the lucky few who hasn't seen my mug on social media, I'm going to explain fully what to do. Leave the potatoes in the colander and place the colander back on the saucepan. Then, place the pan back on the turned-off stove top you just used (you want any residual heat). Place a dish towel on top of the colander to lock in all the steam (don't let the dish towel touch the stove, in case it catches fire – just an FYI). Then, leave the spuds for around 5 minutes, until they are paler around the outside and crumbling away. This is the perfect texture for mashed potatoes or a roasted potato or anything crispy. I use this method a lot throughout this book.

5. Portion by portion, while still hot, pass the steam-dried potatoes and pieces of the butter through a strainer or potato ricer into a bowl, or mash with a potato masher. Adding the butter at the same time coats the starchy particles to keep them fluffy.

6. Warm the cream (in a microwave or on the stove) to the same-ish temperature as the spuds, then add it to the bowl. Stir to just combine (less stirring = less elasticated mash). Welcome to super-smooth, beautiful mashed potatoes.

Mashed Potatoes

GARLIC + THYME MASHED POTATOES

1¼ lbs Yukon Gold
  potatoes

neutral oil

½ cup plant-based
  heavy or whipping
  cream

2 garlic cloves,
  bashed but left
  whole

4 thyme sprigs

3 Tbsp plant-based
  butter, cubed

salt and white
  pepper

First, this is a delicious mashed potato dish. But second,
it's actually plant-based. I know what you're thinking...
PLANT-BASED mash?! Gone are the days where the only
plant-based option was a side salad or a stuffed pepper.
We're delivering indulgent sides without a lettuce leaf in sight.
I did add a customary sprinkling of thyme though... for health.
Of course, for a non-vegan version you can swap out the
plant-based butter and cream for the usual stuff.

————

1. Heat your oven to 425°F and rub your potatoes with oil and salt. Bake the
    potatoes in the oven for 50–60 minutes, until tender all through. We are
    cooking our potatoes this way so that we aren't adding any extra liquid to the
    potatoes – we want it to be drier than a non-vegan mash.

2. Warm your cream and garlic together in a small saucepan on a low heat
    for 8 minutes, until the cream has thickened. Throw in 2 of the thyme sprigs
    and leave to infuse for 5 minutes. Season heavily with salt and pepper and
    keep warm until needed.

3. Slice the baked potatoes in half and scoop out the middles. Use a ricer if you
    have one, or use a spatula to push the cooked potato through a fine-meshed
    strainer to make a very fine mash, into a bowl, adding the plant-based butter
    as you go, to make a very smooth mash.

4. Remove the sprigs and garlic from the warm, infused cream and, using
    a rubber spatula, fold it into the mash. Season well with salt and pepper.
    Strip the rest of the thyme leaves into the mashed potatoes and mix through.

THREE-CHEESE MASHED POTATOES

1¼ lbs Yukon Gold
  potatoes, peeled
  and sliced into
  ¾-inch rounds

½ cup shredded
  mozzarella

½ cup shredded
  extra-sharp cheddar

½ cup shredded
  mild cheddar

3 Tbsp butter

3–5 Tbsp heavy
  cream

salt and white
  pepper

Please welcome to the stage the best friend of every potato… CHEESE. And while we're at it, let's bring in not just one cheese, but three. A ménage à trois of cheeses, lovingly caressed within a velvety smooth mash. All singing in harmony as they make sweet cheesy music with those spuds. Is anyone else feeling a bit hot under the collar? No, just me.

———

1. Put the potato slices into a saucepan of heavily salted, cold water and bring to a boil. Reduce the heat and leave on a gentle boil for around 20 minutes, until the slices fall off the tip of a knife. Drain in a colander.

2. Put the colander back on the empty pan on the turned-off stove top, cover the potatoes with a clean dish towel and leave them to steam-dry for 5 minutes (see page 16).

3. Meanwhile, in a small saucepan over a low heat, melt together the cheeses and butter with 3 Tbsp of the heavy cream. Season well with salt and pepper.

4. Portion by portion, while still hot, pass the steam-dried potatoes through a strainer or potato ricer into a bowl, or mash with a potato masher.

5. Fold the cream mixture into the potatoes while both are still hot, so they combine properly. If the mash is looking a bit thick, warm the remaining cream and add that, too. Taste for seasoning and adjust as necessary.

HOT HONEY + BACON MASHED POTATOES

1¼ lbs Yukon Gold potatoes, peeled and sliced into ¾-inch rounds

5 Tbsp heavy cream

1 garlic clove, minced

1 rosemary sprig

3 Tbsp butter, cubed

½ cup finely grated extra-sharp cheddar, plus extra for the topping

1 heaping tsp Dijon mustard, plus ½ Tbsp for the topping

2 Tbsp honey

1 red chili (such as Fresno) sliced

1 thyme sprig, leaves picked

4 slices of smoked bacon

Hot honey and bacon needs to be on everything. It's sweet, spicy, cheesy, creamy and every other positive adjective you can think of. A bit of spice in your mash never hurt anybody and here the twist brings the perfect balance for your spud. You'll feel a bit trendy with this one, like you're in an East London pub trying to finish a pale ale because it had a cool logo even though you'd rather just have had a lager.

——

1. Put the potato slices into a saucepan of heavily salted, cold water and bring to a boil. Reduce the heat and leave on a gentle boil for around 20 minutes, until the slices fall off the tip of a knife. Drain in a colander.

2. Put the colander back on the empty pan on the turned-off stove top, cover the potatoes with a clean dish towel and leave them to steam-dry for 5 minutes (see page 16).

3. Warm the cream, garlic and rosemary together in a small saucepan over a medium heat until thickened and hot. Season well with salt and pepper.

4. Portion by portion, while still hot, pass the steam-dried potatoes with pieces of the butter through a strainer or potato ricer into a bowl, or mash them together with a potato masher.

5. Remove the rosemary sprig from the warm, infused cream and, using a rubber spatula, fold the cream into the potatoes. Throw in the cheddar and heaping tsp of Dijon and mix together.

6. In a small saucepan, mix together the honey, sliced chili, thyme leaves and the ½ Tbsp of Dijon. Warm them gently for 5 minutes to infuse the honey, then remove the pan from the heat.

7. Heat the oven to 400°F.

8. Meanwhile, in a frying pan over a medium heat, fry the bacon for 8 minutes, until crispy, then chop it up. Stir three-quarters of the chopped bacon through the mashed potatoes, then save the rest for sprinkling later.

9. Spoon the mash into a small baking dish, leveling it out. Pour over the honey mixture, then sprinkle over the reserved bacon and some extra cheddar. Put the dish in the oven for 10–15 minutes, until the cheese is gratinated and bubbling.

CHEESY LEEKY MASHED POTATOES

1¼ lbs Yukon Gold
  potatoes, peeled
  and sliced into
  ¾-inch rounds

1 leek

7 Tbsp butter, plus
  a little to make
  the garnish

3–7 Tbsp heavy
  cream

½ cup shredded
  extra-sharp
  cheddar

salt and white
  pepper

If you haven't confited a leek, prepare to have your mind blown. The caramelized flavors are achieved by submerging your leeks in butter and softening until sweet and tender. Just beautiful, and even better when encased in creamy mash.

———

1. Put the potato slices into a saucepan of heavily salted, cold water and bring to a boil. Reduce the heat and leave on a gentle boil for around 20 minutes, until the slices fall off the tip of a knife. Drain in a colander.

2. Put the colander back on the empty pan on the turned-off stove top, cover the potatoes with a clean dish towel and leave them to steam-dry for 5 minutes (see page 16).

3. Meanwhile, slice the leek in half lengthways, then slice along the lengths into thin pieces, keeping the green and white parts separate. We'll use the green parts later for garnish.

4. Melt the butter in a small saucepan over a low heat and add the white leeks. Leave to cook slowly for 15–20 minutes, until they are soft.

5. Portion by portion, while still hot, pass the steam-dried potatoes through a strainer or potato ricer into a bowl, or mash with a potato masher.

6. Tip the softened leeks and all of the melted butter into the potatoes and, using a rubber spatula, fold them through to evenly combine.

7. Warm 3 Tbsp of the cream and all the cheddar in a small saucepan over a low heat just until the cheese has melted. Gradually incorporate the mixture into the potatoes. If the mashed potatoes are too thick, warm the remaining cream and add it little by little, as needed, until you have the perfect consistency. Taste and season with salt and pepper.

8. To serve, simply melt a little more butter in a frying pan over a medium heat. Once the butter is foaming, add the green slices of leek and cook for 2 minutes, until soft. Drizzle this over your mashed potatoes for a little greenery.

PO-TAY-TOES

Boil 'em,
Mash 'em,
Stick 'em
in a Stew.

BEEFY MASHED POTATOES

1¼ lbs Yukon Gold
potatoes, peeled
and sliced into
¾-inch rounds

2 tsp beef bouillon
concentrate or
1 beef bouillon cube
made into a paste
with 2 Tbsp of
boiling water

2 Tbsp butter

2 Tbsp beef tallow
or extra butter

7 Tbsp heavy cream

2 thyme sprigs

1 rosemary sprig

1 garlic clove, peeled
and bashed but left
whole

1–3 tsp horseradish
sauce, to taste

small bunch of
chives, finely
chopped

salt and white
pepper

Want to make roast beef even more iconically British? Get this mash on your plate. For those who believe mashed potatoes don't belong on with roast beef, please put this book down and have a long hard look at yourself, then pick it back up and get some potatoes on to boil.

For my veggie friends, just swap the beef bouillon for vegetable bouillon and the beef tallow for more butter. You can never go wrong with more butter.

———

1. Put the potato slices into a saucepan of lightly salted, cold water. Add the bouillon, bring the liquid up to a boil, then simmer for around 20 minutes, until the slices fall off the tip of a knife. Drain in a colander.

2. Put the colander back on the empty pan on the turned-off stove top, cover the potatoes with a clean dish towel and leave them to steam-dry for 5 minutes (see page 16).

3. Meanwhile, in a small saucepan over a medium–low heat, add the butter, beef tallow, cream, thyme, rosemary and garlic, and the horseradish sauce to taste. Season well with salt and pepper, and leave to warm through and infuse for 10 minutes. Taste again once the mixture is warm and add more horseradish sauce, if you fancy it.

4. Portion by portion, while still hot, pass the steam-dried potatoes through a strainer or potato ricer into a bowl, or mash with a potato masher.

5. Remove the herbs and garlic from the warm, infused cream and, using a rubber spatula, fold the cream into the potatoes. Taste for seasoning, then fold the chives through.

BBQ RIPPLE MASHED POTATOES

1¼ lbs Yukon Gold
  potatoes, peeled
  and sliced into
  ¾-inch rounds

5 Tbsp heavy cream

3 Tbsp butter

½ cup shredded
  extra-sharp
  cheddar

2 Tbsp BBQ sauce,
  plus optional extra
  to serve

salt and white
  pepper

TO GARNISH

1–2 Tbsp store-
  bought crispy fried
  onions

small bunch of
  chives, finely
  chopped

small handful of
  finely grated
  parmesan

The beautiful rippling of the BBQ sauce cuts through the cheesy sea of mashed potatoes and is a delight for both the eyes and the mouth. I can finally say that I understand art appreciation. Please send this to my art teacher in school and let them know that, yes, I achieved something.

____

1. Put the potato slices into a saucepan of heavily salted, cold water and bring to a boil. Reduce the heat and leave on a gentle boil for around 20 minutes, until the slices fall off the tip of a knife. Drain in a colander.

2. Put the colander back on the empty pan on the turned-off stove top, cover the potatoes with a clean dish towel and leave them to steam-dry for 5 minutes (see page 16).

3. Meanwhile, in a small saucepan, warm the cream with the butter, seasoned with plenty of salt and pepper, over a low heat, until the butter has melted.

4. Portion by portion, while still hot, pass the steam-dried potatoes through a strainer or potato ricer into a bowl, or mash with a potato masher. Using a rubber spatula, fold through the warm cream mixture and the cheese and season again to taste.

5. Pour in the BBQ sauce and ripple it through with the spatula – just ripple, don't mix it entirely. Spoon the mashed potatoes into serving dishes and sprinkle over the crispy onions, chopped chives and grated parmesan, to garnish. Squeeze over some extra BBQ sauce, too, if you wish.

ULTIMATE CHICKEN + TRUFFLE POMME PURÉE

1¼ lbs Yukon Gold potatoes

olive oil

3 chicken skins (you can get these from your local butcher or buy a package of chicken thighs and remove the skin)

2 Tbsp butter

7 Tbsp heavy cream

2 garlic cloves, peeled and bashed but left whole

1 rosemary sprig

1 thyme sprig

2–3 Tbsp good-quality truffle oil, to taste, plus extra if needed

salt and white pepper

I'm seriously considering a mashed-potato bar at my wedding... and a three-tier potato cake... and a Mr Potato Head officiant. You know what, forget the confetti, I want to be showered in parmesan and truffle shavings while we sashay down the aisle. I need to be stopped.

This dish would be *perfect* at a wedding because it's just that little bit more fancy. It's the private members' club of the potato world. Cook this mash and it'll ask you to pay for a monthly subscription just so you can have a spoonful. It's élite, but it knows it's worth it.

———

1. Heat your oven to 425°F and rub your potatoes with oil and salt. Bake the potatoes in the oven for 50–60 minutes, until tender all through.

2. About 30 minutes before the potatoes are done, line a baking sheet with parchment paper and lay the chicken skins out flat. Drizzle them with olive oil and season them well with salt and pepper. Place another piece of parchment paper on top, then top that with another baking sheet or something else ovenproof and heavy so that the skins are completely squashed.

3. Put the chicken skins into the oven and bake them for about 30 minutes, until golden brown and crispy. Place them on a wire rack to cool. Roughly chop about half of the skins, but keep some whole, to garnish.

4. In a small saucepan, mix together the butter, cream, garlic, rosemary, thyme, and truffle oil to taste. Place the pan over a medium heat and leave the mixture to infuse for 5 minutes. Taste and season well with salt and pepper, adding in a bit more truffle oil to your preference, if you like. Keep warm.

5. Slice the baked potatoes in half and scoop out the middles (you can use the skins for any of the recipes on pages 176–185). Use a ricer if you have one, or use a spatula to push the cooked potato through a fine-meshed strainer into a bowl, to make a very fine mash.

6. Remove the whole herbs and garlic from the warm, infused cream and fold the cream through the potatoes. Taste and adjust the seasoning, adding more salt, pepper and truffle oil, if needed.

7. When you're ready to serve, fold through the chopped crispy chicken skin (it'll go soggy if you add it too early), then top the pomme purée with the reserved whole pieces, to garnish.

Serves 4

CHRISTMAS MASHED POTATOES WITH CRISPY BRUSSELS SPROUTS + BACON

1¾ lbs Yukon Gold potatoes, peeled and sliced into ¾-inch rounds

1 chicken bouillon cube

7 Tbsp heavy cream

2 rosemary sprigs

3 Tbsp butter, cubed, plus optional extra for the Brussels sprouts

neutral oil

4 slices thick-cut bacon, diced

1½ cups thinly shredded Brussels sprouts or savoy cabbage leaves

4–6 sage leaves, finely chopped, plus extra to finish

6 oz brie, sliced

drizzle of honey

salt and white pepper

You know what, if you're a sprout-hater, it's because you haven't had sprouts in the best form yet. Don't just boil them and leave them on the side of your Christmas dinner, put them in your mash instead. Plus, we all know that you've gotta eat your greens to make it on to Santa's nice list, so tuck them away within this festive delight and sleigh that five-a-day. Shantay – you sleigh!

———

1. Put the potatoes into a large saucepan of lightly salted, cold water. Add the bouillon cube and bring to a boil. Reduce the heat and leave on a gentle boil for about 20 minutes, until the slices fall off the tip of a knife. Drain in a colander.

2. Put the colander back on the empty pan on the turned-off stove top, cover the potatoes with a clean dish towel and leave them to steam-dry for 5 minutes (see page 16).

3. Meanwhile, in a small saucepan, warm the cream and rosemary, seasoned with plenty of salt and pepper, over a low heat.

4. Portion by portion, while still hot, pass the steam-dried potatoes through a strainer or potato ricer into a bowl, or mash with a potato masher. Remove the rosemary from the warmed, infused cream and, using a rubber spatula, fold the cream through the potatoes. Season to taste, then fold through the butter, until melted.

5. Heat a drizzle of oil in a medium frying pan over a high heat. Add the diced bacon and fry for 5 minutes, until crispy and golden. Add the shredded sprouts (or cabbage) and the sage, and fry for 2–3 minutes, until the greens are cooked. Chuck in a pat of butter, if you fancy!

6. Heat the oven to 400°F.

7. Fold the bacon mixture through the mash and spoon the mash into a baking dish. Arrange the sliced brie over the top, then drizzle the brie with honey, scatter over a few extra sage leaves, and put the whole lot in the oven for 10–15 minutes, until the cheese is oozy and bubbling.

Mashed Potatoes

Chapter Two

Roasted Potatoes

Serves 4

THE CLASSIC ROASTED POTATOES

1¾ lbs Yukon Gold
  potatoes, peeled
  and quartered

7 Tbsp neutral oil

salt

The roasted potato is arguably Britain's favorite potato of all time. It's crispy, it's fluffy, it's delicious. It ticks all the boxes. And I'll go out on a limb and say it's my FAVORITE WAY TO EAT POTATOES. There, I said it. Wow, I can't take that one back.

Is there anything better in the world than dipping your deliciously perfect roasted potatoes into thick, luscious gravy and crunching through into fluffy potato heaven? Okay, now I'm salivating. Just make sure you make enough for seconds... and thirds.

───

1. Get your potatoes into a saucepan of heavily salted, cold water. Place the pan over a high heat, bring the water to a boil and boil the potatoes for 10–15 minutes, until they fall off the tip of a knife. You don't want them too mushy as they won't hold their shape when they roast. Drain in a colander.

2. Leave the potatoes in the colander, over the pan on the turned-off stove top, to steam-dry with a dish towel over the top for 10–15 minutes. This makes them extra-fluffy!

3. Meanwhile, heat the oven to 450°F and get the oil into a rimmed baking sheet. Put the sheet in the oven to get the oil hot.

4. Once the spuds have steam-dried, give them a good toss in the colander to fluff them up, then carefully tip them into the baking sheet with the hot oil.

5. Roast those beauties for 20 minutes, then remove the sheet from the oven. Turn the heat down to 400°F. Give the potatoes a turn and return them to the oven for 30 minutes, until golden and crunchy. You may need less or more time, so keep an eye out.

6. Remove the perfect spuds from the oven, sprinkle them with a little salt, and your ultimate roasted potatoes are ready to go!

WINE + SHALLOT ROASTED POTATOES

1¾ lbs Yukon Gold potatoes, peeled and quartered

1 vegetable bouillon cube

7 Tbsp neutral oil

generous ¾ cup white wine

½ shallot, finely diced

3 garlic cloves, finely chopped

3 Tbsp butter, cubed

2 rosemary sprigs, leaves finely chopped

2 thyme sprigs, leaves finely chopped

salt and black pepper

This is the roasted potato's fancier sister, who comes home for the holidays and judges the whole family. It's a posh one – but so, so delicious. Serve these up as a side for your next BBQ – they are great with some marinated chicken skewers.

There may be a boat-load of flavors going on in this potato dish, but they all complement one another beautifully without any of them overpowering. And, as I'm a big believer in minimal waste, this is a great way to use up any leftover wine. Glass while you prep, glass while you cook, glass while you eat... you get the picture.

———

1. Get your potatoes into a saucepan of cold water, crumble in the bouillon cube and season with a touch of salt. Place the pan over a high heat and bring the water to a boil. Reduce the heat and leave the potatoes on a gentle boil for 10–15 minutes, until they fall off the tip of a knife. Drain in a colander.

2. Leave the potatoes in the colander, over the pan on the turned-off stove top, to steam-dry with a dish towel over the top for 10–15 minutes.

3. Meanwhile, heat the oven to 450°F and get the oil into a rimmed baking sheet. Put the sheet in the oven to get the oil hot.

4. Once the spuds have steam-dried, carefully add them to the hot oil in the baking sheet. Put the potatoes in the oven for 20 minutes, then remove the sheet from the oven. Turn the heat down to 400°F. Give the potatoes a turn and return them to the oven for 30 minutes, until golden and crunchy. You may need less or more time, so keep an eye out.

5. During the last 15 minutes of the potato roasting time, make your reduction. Get a large, high-sided frying pan (like a sauté pan) and add the wine, shallot and garlic. Place this over a high heat and bring the liquid to a rapid boil, leaving it to boil until reduced by about half. Then, reduce the heat and, little by little, whisk in the butter and chopped herbs, until you have a velvety sauce.

6. Toss the potatoes in the saucy reduction and season with salt and black pepper. Enjoy!

MARMITE ROASTED POTATOES

1¾ lbs Yukon Gold
  potatoes, peeled
  and quartered

2 Tbsp Marmite

pinch of salt

7 Tbsp neutral oil

Marmite may be notorious for dividing Britain, but that ends now. Whether a lover or a hater, everyone can find common ground with these amazing spuds. I'll tell you why: the addition of that sticky Marmite isn't overpowering in the slightest – it simply wraps the crispy, golden potatoes in a deep, umami flavor that complements the subtle sweetness of the roasted potato. It's impossible to dislike these roasted potatoes and I ask even the most Marmite devout hater to give them a go – they are little pops of umami goodness and are the perfect side to a steak with a delicious peppercorn sauce.

——

1. Get your potatoes into a saucepan of cold water. Add 1 Tbsp of the Marmite and the pinch of salt. Place the pan over a high heat and bring the water to a boil. Reduce the heat and leave the potatoes on a gentle boil for 10–15 minutes, until they fall off the tip of a knife. You don't want them too mushy as they won't hold their shape when they roast. Drain in a colander (reserve the pan – you're going to use it again).

2. Leave the potatoes in the colander, over the pan on the turned-off stove top, to steam-dry with a dish towel over the top for 10–15 minutes.

3. Meanwhile, heat the oven to 400°F and get the oil into a rimmed baking sheet. Put the sheet in the oven to get the oil hot.

4. Spoon the remaining Marmite into a small bowl and microwave it for 15–30 seconds, just so that it thins slightly and it's easier to coat your potatoes in it.

5. Once the spuds have steam-dried, tip them with the melted Marmite into the reserved saucepan and toss the potatoes to fluff them up. Then, carefully tip them into the baking sheet with the hot oil.

6. Roast them in the oven for 30 minutes, then give them a turn and roast for a further 15–20 minutes, until dark golden and crunchy. If they are sticking to the bottom of the sheet at the 30-minute point, just leave them a little longer before turning – they will unstick when they are ready. Now, because of the Marmite, they will look darker than the usual roasted potato, but don't worry – that's all good. Remove them from the oven and these little babies are ready to go.

LEMON ROASTED POTATOES

1¾ lbs Yukon Gold potatoes, peeled and sliced into ½-inch rounds

1 chicken or vegetable bouillon cube, plus 3 Tbsp chicken or vegetable broth for coating

7 Tbsp neutral oil

2 lemons, 1 juiced and 1 sliced

2 tsp dried oregano

1 garlic clove, minced

2 tsp semolina flour

salt and black pepper

handful of chopped Italian parsley leaves, to serve (optional)

I'm the kinda gal who enjoys a Sunday dinner all year round. I don't care if there's a 100°F heat wave, that chicken is still into the oven. To make it slightly more seasonal, I LOVE to throw in a lemony twist and these roasted potatoes work perfectly. Enjoy your Sunday dinner on a spring or summer's eve in the garden with a big ol' pitcher of white-wine sangria. Bet you're sold now. Maybe we need a potato + wine pairing list...

———

1. Get your potatoes into a saucepan of cold water. Crumble in your bouillon cube and season with a touch of salt. Place the pan over a high heat and bring the water to a boil. Reduce the heat and leave the potatoes on a gentle boil for 10 minutes, until they fall off the tip of a knife. Drain in a colander.

2. Leave the potatoes in the colander, over the pan on the turned-off stove top, to steam-dry with a dish towel over the top for 10–15 minutes.

3. Meanwhile, heat the oven to 400°F and get the oil into a rimmed baking sheet. Put the sheet in the oven to get the oil hot.

4. Once the spuds have steam-dried, give them a good toss in the colander to fluff them up, then carefully tip them into the baking sheet with the hot oil. Place the sheet in the oven to roast the potatoes.

5. Meanwhile, in a bowl, mix the 3 Tbsp of broth with the lemon juice, oregano, garlic and semolina, and season the mixture with salt and pepper.

6. Once your potatoes have been roasting for 30 minutes, take them out of the oven and turn up the heat to 425°F.

7. Pour the lemony liquid over the potatoes, and arrange the lemon slices under the potatoes so the slices do not burn. Then, keep roasting for a further 30 minutes, or until the potatoes are golden and crispy. Season with salt and pepper and sprinkle with some parsley for a final flourish, if you like.

BEEF-, DUCK-, LAMB- OR GOOSE-FAT ROASTIES

1¾ lbs Yukon Gold potatoes, peeled and quartered

pinch of salt

2 tsp beef, chicken or lamb bouillon concentrate or 1 beef, chicken or lamb bouillon cube made into a paste with 2 Tbsp of boiling water, depending on which fat you're using

3–4 Tbsp beef tallow or duck, lamb or goose fat

nice pinch of flaky sea salt, to serve

Okay, I know I've said I like it simple – and now is the level-up. Adding a fat element to your spuds really does give an extra layer of flavor for those days you fancy something a bit special. This recipe is one for when you've got guests coming round who you want to impress. Fat for the win.

____

1. Get your potatoes into a saucepan of cold water with the pinch of salt and add your bouillon (if you're making beef-fat roasties, use beef bouillon, if you're using lamb fat use a lamb bouillon, and if you are using duck or goose fat, use chicken bouillon). Place the pan over a high heat and bring the liquid to a boil. Reduce the heat a little and leave the potatoes to boil gently for 10–15 minutes, until they fall off the tip of a knife. Drain in a colander.

2. Leave the potatoes in the colander, over the pan on the turned-off stove top, to steam-dry with a dish towel over the top for 10–15 minutes.

3. Meanwhile, heat the oven to 425°F. Get your fat of choice into a rimmed baking sheet and place it in the oven to get hot.

4. Once the spuds have steam-dried, give them a good toss in the colander to fluff them up, then carefully tip them into the baking sheet with the melted, hot fat.

5. Put the potatoes in the oven for 20 minutes, then remove the sheet from the oven. Turn the heat down to 400°F. Give the potatoes a turn and return them to the oven for 30 minutes, until golden and crunchy. You may need less or more time, so keep an eye out. Serve sprinkled with flaky sea salt.

When Life Gives You Potatoes, Make a Big ol' Bowl of Roasties.

SOY + GARLIC ROASTED POTATOES

Serves 4

1¾ lbs Yukon Gold potatoes, peeled and quartered

7 Tbsp neutral oil

pinch of crushed red pepper flakes

2½ Tbsp dark soy sauce

2 Tbsp toasted sesame oil

2 garlic cloves, sliced

½ tsp grated fresh ginger

2 scallions, thinly sliced, green and white parts separated

large pinch of flaky sea salt

1 red chili, sliced, to serve

This is the book to make the world realize that so many different flavors can work with potatoes, and I really do hope you try them all and let me know your favorite. This Asian twist on roasted potatoes is absolutely mouth-watering. Soy and garlic work wonders with a spud. Try them once and you might never go back to the classics.

———

1. Get your potatoes into a saucepan of heavily salted, cold water. Place the pan over a high heat and bring the water to a boil. Reduce the heat and leave the potatoes on a gentle boil for 10–15 minutes, until they fall off the tip of a knife. Drain in a colander.

2. Leave the potatoes in the colander, over the pan on the turned-off stove top, to steam-dry with a dish towel over the top for 10–15 minutes.

3. Meanwhile, heat your oven to 425°F and get the oil into a rimmed baking sheet. Put the sheet into the oven to get the oil hot.

4. Once the spuds have steam-dried, give them a good toss in the colander to fluff them up, then carefully tip them into the baking sheet with the hot oil. Place the sheet in the oven to roast the potatoes.

5. Meanwhile, in a bowl, mix together the red pepper flakes, dark soy sauce, sesame oil, garlic, ginger, green parts of the scallions and flaky sea salt.

6. Once your potatoes have been roasting for 30 minutes, take them out of the oven and pour the soy mixture all over the top. Given them a toss and return them to the oven for 15–20 minutes, until golden and crunchy all over.

7. Serve with the sliced red chili and white parts of the scallions sprinkled on top.

Serves 4–6

CHICKEN + STUFFING ROASTIES

1¾ lbs Yukon Gold
  potatoes, peeled
  and quartered

3 garlic cloves,
  peeled

1 chicken bouillon
  cube

7 Tbsp neutral oil

2 rosemary sprigs

2 thyme sprigs

⅔ cup herb-
  seasoned stuffing
  mixture

broth, boiling water,
  butter as needed
  to make up the
  stuffing mix

These are the perfect accompaniment to your weekend chicken roast, because you know what a roast chicken and stuffing needs? More flavors of chicken and stuffing. Yes, please. Let's normalize eating a full bowl of roasted potatoes as a snack and eat them on a Monday, if you really want. Go wild. There's no judgement here.

——

1. Get your potatoes into a saucepan of lightly salted, cold water. Throw in the garlic cloves and crumble in the bouillon cube. Place the pan over a high heat and bring the water to a boil. Reduce the heat and leave the potatoes on a gentle boil for 10–15 minutes, until they fall off the tip of a knife. Drain in a colander over a pitcher – you want to keep the cooking liquid because it's perfect for making gravy later on.

2. Leave the potatoes in the colander, over the pan on the turned-off stove top, to steam-dry with a dish towel over the top for 10–15 minutes.

3. Meanwhile, heat your oven to 425°F and get the oil into a rimmed baking sheet. Put the sheet into the oven to get the oil hot.

4. Once the spuds have steam-dried, chuck them, with the garlic, back into the saucepan and shake them to fluff them up. Then, carefully tip the lot into the baking sheet with the hot oil.

5. Add the rosemary and thyme sprigs to the baking sheet and return it to the oven for 15 minutes, then turn the potatoes over. Give them another 15 minutes, then remove the garlic and herbs.

6. In this time, make up your stuffing mix following the package instructions – but don't bake it.

7. Once the potatoes are ready, push handfuls of stuffing mixture on to the potatoes themselves, almost like you are coating them in stuffing. Be careful as the potatoes will be hot. Once all the potatoes have a little bit of stuffing on them, you can add any remaining stuffing to the baking sheet for extra-crispy pieces.

8. Return the stuffing-coated potatoes to the oven and roast for 15 minutes, until the stuffing is crispy.

52

CHRISTMAS ROASTIES

1¾ lbs Yukon Gold
   potatoes, quartered
   (skin on)

2 Tbsp duck or
   goose fat or
   neutral oil

small handful of
   cooked chestnuts,
   chopped into rough
   chunks

5 slices smoked
   bacon

3 sage leaves, sliced

mature stilton or
   other blue cheese,
   for crumbling
   (optional)

salt and black
   pepper

This is the ultimate roasted potato for Christmas. The extra va-va-voom of chestnuts, sage and bacon will have you wishing it was Christmas every single day. And here's a life hack for you – wrap up one of these roasties for a last-minute gift idea and I can guarantee the recipient will prefer it to a bodywash or a pair of socks. Also, there is nothing to stop you from cooking this every Sunday, because potatoes are for life, not just for Christmas.

——

1. Get your potatoes into a saucepan of heavily salted, cold water. Place the pan over a high heat and bring the water to a boil. Reduce the heat and leave the potatoes on a gentle boil for 10–15 minutes, until they fall off the tip of a knife. Drain in a colander.

2. Leave the potatoes in the colander, over the pan on the turned-off stove top, to steam-dry with a dish towel over the top for 10–15 minutes.

3. Meanwhile, heat the oven to 425°F and get the fat or oil into a rimmed baking sheet. Put the sheet into the oven to get the fat or oil hot.

4. Once the potatoes have steam-dried, add them to the baking sheet with the hot fat or oil, give them a bit of a toss and get them coated in all the fatty goodness. Roast for 35 minutes, giving them a stir twice during roasting. Try not to disrupt them too much, otherwise they may break up.

5. Reduce the heat to 400°F. Add the chestnuts and bacon to the baking sheet and cook for a further 8–10 minutes, until the bacon is crispy. Remove the sheet from the oven and cut the bacon into chunks.

6. Tip everything into a bowl, mix in the sage and season with salt and pepper. Crumble in the stilton, if using, and devour! So festive, so delicious.

Serves 4

SPICED ROASTED POTATOES

1¾ lbs Yukon Gold
  potatoes, peeled
  and quartered

1 garlic clove, peeled
  and bashed but left
  whole

1 chicken bouillon
  cube

3 Tbsp ghee or
  neutral oil

2 tsp black mustard
  seeds

1 tsp cumin seeds

4 fresh curry leaves

3–4-inch cinnamon
  stick, snapped

2 cardamom pods,
  bashed

1 tsp ground turmeric

1 heaping tsp mild
  curry powder

1 Tbsp tomato paste

salt

Plot twist – the possibilities are endless when it comes to roasted potatoes. These spiced beauties are inspired by southern Asian ingredients – think of the flavor combinations you get in an Indian restaurant or takeout. Why not spice up your life with a spicy twist on your favorite roasted potatoes?

————

1. Get the potatoes, garlic clove, chicken bouillon cube and a big pinch of salt in a saucepan of cold water. Place the pan over a high heat and bring the water to a boil. Reduce the heat and leave the potatoes on a gentle boil for 10–15 minutes, until they fall off the tip of a knife. Drain in a colander.

2. Leave the potatoes in the colander, over the pan on the turned-off stove top, to steam-dry with a dish towel over the top for 10–15 minutes.

3. Meanwhile, heat the oven to 450°F and get the ghee or oil into a rimmed baking sheet. Put the sheet into the oven to get the ghee or oil hot.

4. After 10 minutes, throw the mustard seeds, cumin seeds, curry leaves, cinnamon-stick pieces, cardamom pods and turmeric into the baking sheet with the hot fat and leave them until they start to pop and sizzle (about 5 minutes).

5. Once the potatoes have steam-dried, put them back in the saucepan and toss them with the curry powder and tomato paste, until coated. Then, carefully tip them into the sheet of spices and oil and stir them through to get everything coated.

6. Roast the potatoes for 20 minutes, then remove the sheet from the oven. Turn the heat down to 400°F. Give the potatoes a turn and return them to the oven for 30 minutes, until golden and crunchy. You may need less or more time, so keep an eye on them.

Chapter Three

French Fries, Wedges + Hash Browns

CLASSIC FRENCH FRIES

Serves 2

1¾ lbs long, thick
   Yukon Gold
   potatoes (14 oz
   per person)

neutral oil

salt

garlic mayo, to serve
   (optional)

Ahh, the great debates of the Potato Universe. A French fry. Or, as we say here in the UK, a chip. But for my friends across the pond, if I say "chip", you think I am talking about a bag of chips, or as the British call it, a crisp. In which case, just so that I don't cause too much confusion (or offense), I'm calling these slim, thin fried potatoes "French fries". But later on in this chapter there are British Chip-Shop Chips – not as in a bag of chips/crisps, but as in a thicker French fry. Hope this helps. Either way, these babies were first made in Belgium (even though they are called French fries). For that reason, it's only right to have them with some mayo – but not any mayo, a garlic mayo. For this thin French fry, the shape is essential – don't skimp on the precision. Let's be honest, the result has to look like one from the Golden Arches.

──────

1. Leaving the skin on or peeling the spuds for your fries is completely up to you. Now, if you have a mandoline, use this to get that perfect fry shape. If not, carefully cut ¼-inch slices of potato, then get the slices flat and cut ¼-inch-wide lengths – the iconic French-fry shape.

2. Get the fries into a saucepan of heavily salted, cold water. Place the pan over a high heat, bring the water to a boil and boil the fries for 4–5 minutes, until they fall off the tip of a knife. Gently scoop the potatoes out of the water with a slotted spoon so they don't break apart.

3. One by one, spread the fries out over a rack placed in a baking sheet (be careful so as not to break up the fries). Place a dish towel over them and leave them to steam-dry for 5–10 minutes.

4. Pour your oil into a deep fryer or a heavy-based saucepan (don't let it come more than halfway up the inside of the pan). Place the pan over a high heat and get it to 275°F on a candy thermometer (or use the fryer thermometer). In batches, fry the fries for 3–5 minutes, until they have a solid outside – no color, just hard. Remove each batch from the pan carefully and place the fries back on the rack to cool. Once you've finished this first frying, transfer the fries (on the rack in the baking sheet) to the fridge to cool down completely.

5. Meanwhile, get the oil up to 350°F.

6. Once the fries are cold, re-fry them in the hotter oil, until golden and super-crispy – about 2–3 minutes per batch. Set each batch aside to drain on paper towel while you fry the remainder. Once they are all cooked, put them into a bowl, sprinkle with salt, toss, and serve with the mayo, if you like. They are perfection!

Serves 2

CLASSIC THICK-CUT FRIES

1¼ lbs long, thick
  russet potatoes

neutral oil

salt

mustard or ketchup,
  to serve (optional)

For the British, if it's thicker and chunkier, it's definitely a "chip." Or if we're being properly British here, it's a "CHUNKEH chip." (I don't know why that -eh is so important, except it just gives it so much more power. Just saying that makes it sound chunkier.) My American friends may know these as steak fries. And there is something that is a bit fancier about a seriously CHUNKY fry. As you know with me, the chunkier the better.

——

1. Top and tail the potatoes, then cut down each side of each one until they are all square-ish. Peel off any skin that's left. Then, cut each spud into ¾-inch-thick slabs. Turn each slab so that it sits flat and cut it into ¾-inch-thick fries. You should be left with thick-cut fries, all about the size of your index finger (and you can just use your index finger as a measure if you cba with a ruler).

2. Get the fries into a saucepan of heavily salted, cold water. Place the pan over a high heat, bring the water to a boil and boil the fries for 7 minutes, until they fall off the tip of a knife. Gently scoop the potatoes out of the water with a slotted spoon so they don't break apart.

3. One by one, spread the fries out over a rack placed in a baking sheet (be careful so as not to break up the fries). Place a dish towel over them and leave them to steam-dry for 5–10 minutes.

4. Pour your oil into a deep fryer or a heavy-based saucepan (don't let it come more than halfway up the inside of the pan). Place the pan over a high heat and get the oil to 275°F on a candy thermometer (or use the fryer thermometer). In batches, cook the fries for 5–7 minutes, until they have a solid outside – no color, just hard. Remove each batch from the pan carefully and place the fries back on the rack to cool. Once you've finished this first frying, transfer the fries to the fridge (on the rack in the baking sheet) to cool down completely.

5. Meanwhile, get the oil in the pan up to 350°F.

6. Once the fries are cold, re-fry them (in batches) in the hotter oil, until completely golden and tender (about 3–5 minutes). Set each batch aside to drain on paper towel while you fry the remainder. Sprinkle the lot with plenty of salt, and devour – with mustard or ketchup or whatever you fancy.

CRUNCHY BABY FRIES

1¼ lbs long, thick
  Yukon Gold
  potatoes, peeled

neutral oil

salt

OOH, BABY! If you're all about the crunch when it comes to fries, this is the recipe you need in your life. And how cute do baby fries sound? They are also known as "shoestring fries" across the Atlantic. They're not all fluffy and soft, but they don't need to be. They're about adding that crunch to your dish. And because they're so little, you can cook them in half the time. Easy, quick, fried potatoes. I'm a happy gal. I love these babies with a hot dog.

––––––

1. Get a bowl of cold water ready. Cut your potatoes into thin slices, about ⅛ inch thick. Then, cut each potato slice into ⅛-inch sticks, so that you have thin, baby fries – a super-sharp knife will really help. Transfer the potato matchsticks to the water as you go and leave them there until you're ready to cook.

2. Pour enough oil into a deep, large frying pan so that the oil is about 1 inch deep, and place it over a medium–high heat. It's hot enough when the tip of a fry sizzles slightly. You don't want the oil to be too hot because you want the fries to cook and crisp up, not instantly burn.

3. Drain off your fries and carefully add about 2 handfuls of them to the pan. Leave them to cook in the oil, turning occasionally, until they are mostly golden (about 3–5 minutes). Drain them on paper towel while you fry the remaining handfuls, then season with salt. (Warning: try to avoid eating each batch immediately, before you've fried the rest.)

OVEN FRIES

2¼ lbs long, thick
   Yukon Gold
   potatoes, peeled

¼ cup neutral oil

salt

ketchup, to serve
   (optional)

Fried fries are great, but sometimes you might not fancy whapping the oil out. Here's where oven fries steal the show. They are the answer on that evening you just want to bung everything into the oven and still get the crisp that you get from deep-frying. Oven fries need a renaissance because when they're good... they're good. I like these as the "chips" part of "ham, egg and chips", with ketchup. A British classic.

———

1. Slice your potatoes into the perfect fry shape (the thickness of your index finger is always a good measure) and get them into cold water to soak for a few minutes. Then, rinse them off and transfer them to a shallow but wide saucepan of heavily salted, cold water. Place the pan over a high heat and bring the water to a boil. Boil the potatoes for 7 minutes, until they fall off the tip of a knife. Gently scoop the potatoes out of the water with a slotted spoon so they don't break apart.

2. One by one, spread the fries out over a rack placed over a baking sheet (be careful so as not to break up the fries). Place a dish towel over them and leave them to steam-dry for 5–10 minutes.

3. Meanwhile, heat the oven to 425°F and get the oil into a rimmed baking sheet. Put the sheet in the oven to get the oil hot.

4. Once the fries have steam-dried, carefully remove the baking sheet from the oven and tip the fries into it, giving them one little mix so that they get coated in the hot oil but don't break up. Watch your hands for any spitting oil.

5. Return the sheet to the oven for 30–50 minutes (the time depends on how big you sliced your fries), turning halfway through so that all the sides get the opportunity to crisp up. Once the fries are golden and crispy, serve up and enjoy! Maybe with an extra sprinkling of salt and a squirt of ketchup for good measure.

BRITISH CHIP-SHOP CHIPS

1¾ lbs long, thick russet potatoes, peeled

enough beef tallow to fill your saucepan to about 2½ inches deep

salt and malt vinegar, to serve

Hello, my name is Poppy O'Toole and I'm addicted to vinegar. I'm that person who drowns their fries in the stuff, then drinks the remainder. It's awful, I know, but I can't stop. And I won't stop. Now, whack some vinegar on my proper British chip-shop chips and dig in.

I call these beauties "chippie chips" because in parts of the UK going "down the chippie" was a weekly affair to grab your cod or haddock and chips all wrapped up in paper. I understand that to people outside the UK this sounds a bit out there, but us Brits just get it. It's truly a staple. Try making these at home, with some battered haddock (you can even wrap them up in some paper, if you fancy it) and mushy peas for a full "chippie" experience. Beef tallow is the traditional cooking fat for chip-shop chips, but if you can't find it then use neutral oil instead.

———

1. Slice your potatoes into the perfect "chip" shape (a bit thicker than your index finger).

2. Get the potatoes into a saucepan of heavily salted, cold water. Place the pan over a high heat, bring the water to a boil and boil the potatoes for 7 minutes, until they fall off the tip of a knife. Gently scoop the potatoes out of the water with a slotted spoon so they don't break apart.

3. One by one, spread the potatoes out over a rack placed in a baking sheet (be careful so as not to break up the potatoes). Place a dish towel over them and leave them to steam-dry for 5–10 minutes.

4. Add the fat to the saucepan, and heat it to 275°F on a candy thermometer. In batches, fry the potatoes for 5–7 minutes, until they have a solid outside – no color, just hard. Remove each batch from the pan carefully, and place the "chips" back on the rack to cool. Once you've finished this first frying, transfer all the "chips" (on the rack in the baking sheet) to the fridge to cool down completely.

5. Meanwhile, get the fat up to 350°F.

6. Once the "chips" are cold, re-fry them (in batches) in the hotter fat, until completely golden and tender (about 3–5 minutes). Set each batch aside to drain on paper towel while you fry the remainder. Douse in malt vinegar and salt for that perfect chip-shop chip.

ORANGE-BATTERED FRIES

1¾ lbs long, thick Yukon Gold potatoes, peeled

⅓ cup plus 1 Tbsp all-purpose flour, plus extra for coating

5 Tbsp cornstarch

1 tsp turmeric

drop of orange food coloring

1 tsp fine salt

¾ cup–1¼ cups cold lager, as needed

neutral oil

flaky sea salt, to serve

"'Orange chips" are a staple of the West Midlands in England. My grandmother's family were from this region and we'd head down to the famous Bilston Market every week and always end the day with some "orange chips". The orange-ness comes from a dash of turmeric, but you can also add a drop of orange food coloring, as I have here, to really make them POP. Basically, you wanna see them in the dark. The best way to eat these orange chips is straight away with loads of salt and vinegar. Sometimes you just don't mess with a classic.

————

1. Slice your potatoes into the perfect fry shape (the thickness of your index finger is always a good measure).

2. Get the potatoes into a saucepan of heavily salted, cold water. Place the pan over a high heat, bring the water to a boil and boil the chips for 7 minutes, until they fall off the tip of a knife. Gently scoop the potatoes out of the water with a slotted spoon so they don't break apart.

3. One by one, spread the potatoes out over a rack placed over a baking sheet (be careful so as not to break up the potatoes). Place a dish towel over them and leave them to steam-dry for 5–10 minutes.

4. To make the batter, mix the flours, turmeric, coloring and tsp of salt together. Then, stir in the lager, a little at a time, until you have a smooth but thick batter that will stick to the fries but still be light and fluffy. Set aside.

5. Pour your oil into a deep fryer or a heavy-based saucepan (don't let it come more than halfway up the inside of the pan). Place the pan over a high heat and get the oil to 350°F on a candy thermometer (or use the fryer thermometer).

6. Once the potatoes have dried out, toss them in a little more flour to just coat.

7. Lightly dip the potatoes into the batter, then carefully add a few batter-coated potatoes at a time to the hot oil and fry until completely golden all over and the batter has crisped up – this might take longer than you expect, so keep an eye on them. (A safety message for life: never leave a fryer alone!)

8. Carefully scoop the cooked fries from the pan and on to paper towel to absorb any excess oil. Continue to cook in batches until they are all fried, then season with flaky sea salt and eat right there.

SALT 'N' PEPPER FRIES

Serves 2

1¾ lbs long, thick Yukon Gold potatoes, peeled

neutral oil

½ green bell pepper, seeded and cubed

1 red chili, sliced (seeded for less heat)

2 garlic cloves, sliced

1 tsp Chinese five-spice powder

1 Tbsp Lyle's golden syrup or light corn syrup

salt

crushed red pepper flakes, to serve (optional)

Another British thing that has gone viral internationally over the last few years is our love of a Chinese takeout. Salt and pepper fries are a staple of these – and are basically your favorite fried potatoes mixed with delicious peppers and Chinese seasoning to make a must-have every time you order. They're super-easy to make at home, too.

A nice dip to go with this is a lime-and-cilantro number. In a bowl, mix together sour cream, mayonnaise, chopped cilantro, lime juice, lime zest, grated garlic, and salt and pepper to your taste, then chill in the fridge for 30 minutes or so to help all the flavors combine. Serve with your fries.

——

1. Slice your potatoes into the perfect fry shape (the thickness of your index finger is always a good measure).

2. Get the potatoes into a saucepan of heavily salted, cold water. Place the pan over a high heat, bring the water to a boil and boil the potatoes for 7 minutes, until they fall off the tip of a knife. Gently scoop the potatoes out of the water with a slotted spoon so they don't break apart.

3. One by one, spread the potatoes out over a rack placed over a baking sheet (be careful so as not to break up the potatoes). Place a dish towel over them and leave them to steam-dry for 5–10 minutes.

4. Pour your oil into a deep fryer or a heavy-based saucepan (don't let it come more than halfway up the inside of the pan). Place the pan over a high heat and get the oil to 275°F on a candy thermometer (or use the fryer thermometer). In batches, cook the fries for 5–8 minutes, until they have a solid outside – no color, just hard. Remove each batch from the pan carefully and set them aside to drain on paper towel

5. Once all the fries are draining, increase the temperature of the oil to 350°F.

6. In batches again, cook the fries for about 3–5 minutes, until golden, draining each batch on paper towel to soak up any excess oil.

7. In a separate saucepan, heat up 1 Tbsp of oil over a medium–high heat. Add the bell pepper, chili and garlic and fry for 2–3 minutes, to soften, then add the Chinese five-spice and golden syrup. The room should be filled with that beautiful salt 'n' pepper aroma.

8. Chuck the fries into the pan with the pepper mixture and toss together. Season well with salt, sprinkle with red pepper flakes, if you like, then serve up. Enjoy!

POTATO SMILES

1¾ lbs Yukon Gold
  potatoes, peeled
  and quartered

1½ Tbsp cornstarch,
  plus extra if needed

2 tsp garlic powder

1 tsp sweet paprika

neutral oil

salt and black
  pepper

Potato smiles are the British equivalent of Tater Tots. These iconic potato snacks captured the hearts of all of us 90s babies and brought instant happiness to the kitchen table. Well, apart from when you were midway through your math homework, crying because you couldn't work out 8x6. To properly reminisce (minus the math flashbacks), you absolutely must serve these alongside SpaghettiO's and crispy chicken strips. The food of champions.

——

1. Put the potatoes into a saucepan of heavily salted, cold water. Place the pan over a high heat, bring the water to a boil and boil the potatoes for about 15–20 minutes, until they are tender but not mushy. Drain in a colander. Place the colander over the pan on the turned-off stove top, cover with a dish towel and leave to steam-dry for 10–15 minutes (until they are cool enough to handle).

2. Tip three-quarters of the potatoes into a mixing bowl and mash them with a fork or potato masher. Cut the remainder into ¼-inch cubes and stir them through the mash.

3. Add the cornstarch, garlic powder and paprika to the mash, and season with salt and pepper, stirring until you form a soft but not sticky dough (you may need a little extra cornstarch).

4. Using a rolling pin, roll out the dough to around ¾ inch thick, then use a 1½-inch round cookie cutter to cut out as many circles as you can (you'll get about 18-ish). Discard any excess dough. Then, this is the fun part: in each round of potato, use a paper straw or something else small, circular and hollow (like the end of a piping tip) to make two holes for the eyes, and a small, sharp knife to carve out a smile (use the photograph as a guide).

5. Place your potato smiles on a baking sheet lined with parchment paper and put them in the fridge for at least 1 hour to firm up. This will help the smiles keep their shape when fried.

6. Pour your oil into a deep fryer or a heavy-based saucepan (don't let it come more than halfway up the inside of the pan). Place the pan over a high heat and get it to 350°F on a candy thermometer (or use the thermometer in your fryer).

7. In batches, fry the potato smiles for about 2–3 minutes, turning halfway through, until golden brown and crispy all over. Drain each batch on paper towel while you fry the remainder. Be sure to serve with your favorite childhood classics and a big squeeze of ketchup. Let's get nostalgic.

LOADED FRIES ("ANIMAL FRIES" VIBES)

Serves 2

1¾ lbs long, thick Yukon Gold potatoes, peeled

neutral oil

1 large onion, chopped

salt and black pepper

5 slices of American processed cheese

splash of whole milk

FOR THE SAUCY TOPPING

5 Tbsp mayonnaise

2 Tbsp ketchup

1 Tbsp sweet relish

1 tsp white wine vinegar

pinch of sugar

pinch of sweet paprika

pinch of onion powder

pinch of garlic powder

I couldn't be the Potato Queen online without leaning into a few of the viral trends – and trust me when I say I'm fully aware there are a lot of duds out there. At one point, for example, people were boiling salted potato chips to try and recreate mashed potatoes. Those kinda viral recipes will not be featured in this book. Animal fries, on the other hand, are absolutely delicious and a trend worth the hype. Try them for yourself and let me know what you think.

1. Carefully slice your potatoes into fries (see page 60) and put them into a pan of heavily salted, cold water. Place over a high heat and bring the water to a boil. Boil the potatoes for 5–7 minutes, until they fall off the tip of a knife. Gently scoop the potatoes out of the water with a slotted spoon so they don't break.

2. Very gently, spread the potatoes out over a rack placed over a baking sheet (be careful so as not to break up the potatoes). Place a dish towel over them and leave them to steam-dry for 5–10 minutes.

3. Pour your oil into a deep fryer or a heavy-based saucepan (don't let it come more than halfway up the inside of the pan). Place the pan over a high heat and get it to 275°F on a candy thermometer (or use the thermometer in your fryer). In batches, cook the fries for 5–8 minutes, until they have a solid outside – no color, just hard. Remove each batch from the pan and carefully set it back on the wire rack to drain. Leave the last batch of fries to drain while the fryer heats to 350°F.

4. In batches again, return the fries to the oil and fry for 3–5 minutes, until golden and crispy. Drain the fries on paper towel and sprinkle with salt. Place the fries in an ovenproof dish.

5. During the second fry, heat a splash of oil in a frying pan over a medium–high heat. Add the onion. Fry for 10–15 minutes, until golden brown, then season with salt and pepper.

6. In a bowl, microwave the cheese slices and splash of milk until they are melted, and give them a good stir to emulsify them into a sauce. (I know this sounds odd, but it honestly gives the quickest and easiest cinema-style nacho cheese sauce.) Drizzle this all over the fries.

7. In a small bowl, mix together the saucy ingredients, then dollop this all over the fries and scatter with the caramelized onion before you dig in.

MASALA FRIES

1¾ lbs long, thick russet potatoes, peeled

neutral oil

1 Tbsp ghee

1 thumb-sized piece of ginger, grated or minced

2 garlic cloves, finely grated or minced

1 onion, chopped into large dice

1 tsp smoked paprika

½ tsp cayenne pepper

½ tsp ground black pepper

½ tsp ground coriander

½ tsp cumin seeds

1 tsp mild curry powder

TO GARNISH

flaky sea salt

lime wedges

sliced red chili (such as Fresno)

sliced scallions

Growing up in the West Midlands, I was lucky enough to be surrounded by some incredible curry restaurants and spice markets, which really opened my eyes to different flavor profiles and cultures. Here is my take on masala fries. If the ingredient list doesn't seem expansive enough, throw on some yogurt, cilantro and pickled red onions – just because!

———

1. Slice your potatoes into the perfect fry shape (the thickness of your index finger is always a good measure). Put the potatoes into a pan of heavily salted, cold water and place the pan over a high heat. Bring the water to a boil, then reduce the heat and boil gently for 5–8 minutes, until the potatoes are tender but still holding their shape. Gently scoop the potatoes out of the water with a slotted spoon so they don't break apart.

2. Carefully arrange the potatoes in a single layer on a wire rack placed over a baking sheet. Place a dish towel over the top and steam-dry for 10 minutes.

3. Meanwhile, pour your oil into a deep fryer or a heavy-based saucepan (don't let it come more than halfway up the inside of the pan). Place the pan over a high heat and get the oil to 325°F on a candy thermometer (or use the fryer thermometer).

4. In batches, cook the fries for about 3–5 minutes, until they are just blanched – cooked in the middle but pale on the outside. Remove to the wire rack while the oil heats to 350°F.

5. In batches again, give the fries a second fry until golden and crispy – about 3–5 minutes. Remove each batch to drain on paper towel while you fry the remainder.

6. Meanwhile, heat a large frying pan over a medium–high heat and throw in the ghee to melt. Fry the ginger and garlic together until fragrant, then add the onion. Fry for 5–7 minutes, until the onion is softened, then add in all of the spices. Cook for 30 seconds to toast the spices in the ghee.

7. Toss the cooked fries through the spiced onions and ghee, then garnish with a sprinkle of flaky sea salt, wedges of lime and the slices of chili and scallions.

SOUTHERN-FRIED FRIES

Serves 2

1¼ lbs long, thick
    russet potatoes,
    peeled

neutral oil

1¼ cups buttermilk

3 tsp salt

2 tsp smoked
    paprika

1 tsp ground black
    pepper

1 tsp cayenne
    pepper

2 tsp dried oregano

2 tsp garlic powder

2 tsp onion powder

1⅔ cups all-purpose
    flour

flaky sea salt, to
    serve

FOR THE DIP

1 Tbsp sour cream

½ Tbsp mayonnaise

1 Tbsp buttermilk

1 garlic clove, minced

salt and black
    pepper

This one goes out to everyone's favorite Kentucky uncle. He might know his way around his chicken – but someone needs to seriously ask him why he hasn't been Southern frying his fries. Serve these babies with a big ol' piece of fried chicken, homemade coleslaw and a cheeky corn-on-the-cob.

———

1. Carefully slice your potatoes into fries (see page 60) and put them into a pan of heavily salted, cold water. Place the pan over a high heat, bring the water to a boil, then boil the fries for 5–7 minutes, until they fall off the tip of a knife. Gently scoop the potatoes out of the water with a slotted spoon so they don't break apart.

2. Carefully arrange the potatoes in a single layer on a wire rack set over a baking sheet (be careful not to break up the potatoes). Place a dish towel over them and leave them to steam-dry for 10 minutes.

3. Meanwhile, pour your oil into a deep fryer or a heavy-based saucepan (don't let it come more than halfway up the inside of the pan). Place the pan over a high heat and get the oil to 325°F on a candy thermometer (or use the thermometer in your fryer).

4. Make the dip while you wait for the oil to heat up – simply combine the dip ingredients in a bowl, season with salt and pepper and set aside.

5. In batches, cook the fries for about 4–6 minutes, until they have a solid outside – no color, just hard. Remove each batch and carefully set it back on the wire rack to drain. Leave the last batch to drain while the fryer heats to 350°F.

6. In a large bowl, mix together the buttermilk and half the salt and half of all the seasonings, herbs and spices. Add the fries to the buttermilk mixture and leave them to soak while you prepare the flour.

7. Whisk the rest of the seasonings, herbs and spices into the flour and use your fingers to sprinkle over a little of the buttermilk mixture, stirring through to form some clumps of flour that will go super-crunchy. Gently scoop the fries from the buttermilk mixture and toss them through the flour to get an uneven, knobbly coating.

8. In batches, cook the fries in the hotter oil for 2–4 minutes, until the flour is golden and crispy. Set aside each batch to drain on paper towel while you fry the remainder. Once you have cooked all the fries, finish with a final sprinkling of flaky sea salt. Serve with the dip.

Serves 4

CLASSIC SKIN-ON WEDGES (OR WEDGIES)

1¾ lbs Yukon Gold potatoes (skin on), cut into large wedges (about 8 wedges per potato)

3 Tbsp neutral oil

1 tsp dried rosemary

1 tsp garlic powder

1 tsp onion powder

1 tsp crushed red pepper flakes

1 tsp cumin seeds

1 tsp cayenne pepper

1 Tbsp cornstarch

1 chicken bouillon cube, crumbled

salt and black pepper

So, I very recently found out that not everyone calls these POTATO WEDGIES! Apparently, it's "potato wedges"? Not wedgies?!?? Not sure I should be admitting that as a professional chef with ten years' experience, but I'm genuinely shook. Have people just been too polite to correct me all this time...? I'm sticking with it, though. These wedgies go perfectly with a classic club sandwich. All you need is bread, chicken breast, bacon, egg, lettuce, tomato and mayo – then have yourself a bowl of wedgies and enjoy.

_____

1. Get your wedges into a saucepan of heavily salted, cold water. Place the pan over a high heat and bring the water to a boil. Boil the wedges for 7–10 minutes, until they fall off the tip of a knife. Drain in a colander. Leave the wedges in the colander, placed over the pan on the turned-off stove top, to steam-dry with a dish towel over the top for 5–10 minutes.

2. Meanwhile, heat the oven to 400°F and get the oil into a rimmed baking sheet. Put the sheet into the oven to get the oil hot.

3. Mix together all the other ingredients in a bowl, season with salt and pepper, and scatter the mixture over the dried-out wedges. Turn the wedges to coat them evenly.

4. Carefully tip the wedges into the baking sheet with the hot oil and roast for 50–60 minutes, turning halfway through, until crispy and piping hot. Just the way I like it.

CAJUN-SPICED WEDGES

1¾ lbs Yukon Gold
  potatoes (skin
  on), cut into large
  wedges (about
  8 wedges per
  potato)

3 Tbsp neutral oil

1 Tbsp Cajun
  seasoning

½ tsp celery salt

1 Tbsp cornstarch

salt and black
  pepper

This is a super-simple way to give classic wedges that extra bit of oomph. I think wedges often get a bad rep as the less successful family member of fries and potato chips. But, you know what? Wedges have their place and they deserve to shine. Let's take a moment to appreciate the wedge in all its glory. You're doing good, kid. We love you, too.

----

1. Get your wedges into a saucepan of heavily salted, cold water. Place the pan over a high heat and bring the water to a boil. Boil the wedges for 7–10 minutes, until they fall off the tip of a knife. Drain in a colander. Leave the wedges in the colander, placed over the pan on the turned-off stove top, to steam-dry with a dish towel over the top for 5–10 minutes.

2. Meanwhile, heat the oven to 400°F and get the oil into a rimmed baking sheet. Put the sheet into the oven to get the oil hot.

3. Mix all the other ingredients in a bowl with a pinch of black pepper to create a seasoning and scatter the seasoning over the wedges. Turn the wedges to coat evenly.

4. Carefully tip the wedges into the baking sheet with the hot oil and roast for 50–60 minutes, turning halfway through, until crispy and piping hot.

BAKED POTATO WEDGES

1¾ lbs Yukon Gold
  potatoes

neutral oil

salt

**SERVING
SUGGESTIONS**

1 cup shredded
  extra-sharp
  cheddar

2 slices of smoked
  bacon, cooked
  until crispy, then
  crumbled

2 Tbsp sour cream

1 red chili (such as
  Fresno), sliced

2 scallions, sliced

A baked potato wedge? Yes, you heard it right. This is like the cronut of the potato world. The ultimate hybrid. And it's so, so good. I've yet to finish a bowl of these cheesy, loaded wedges without dropping at least one down myself. They're a tad on the messy side, but grab a bib, tie your hair back and maybe eat them in private. You won't wanna share anyway, tbh.

———

1. Heat the oven to 425°F.

2. Rub your potatoes with oil and salt and pierce them all over with a fork. Bake the potatoes in the oven, directly on the rack, for 50–60 minutes, until tender, then slice them each into 8 wedges and leave them to dry out while you prepare the oil for deep-frying.

3. Pour your oil into a deep fryer or a heavy-based saucepan (don't let it come more than halfway up the inside of the pan). Place the pan over a high heat and get it to 350°F on a candy thermometer (or use the thermometer in your fryer). In batches, fry the wedges until golden – about 2–3 minutes per batch. Keep an eye on them as they can color quite fast! Drain each batch on paper towel while you fry the remainder. Sprinkle with salt.

4. You can eat them just like that, dunked in your favorite ketchup, or you can add some toppings and get them all oozy. To do this, place the wedges in an ovenproof dish in a single layer. Top with the shredded cheddar and crumbled bacon. Put under a hot broiler and broil until the cheese is oozy and delicious. Then, remove from the broiler, spoon over the sour cream and sprinkle with the red chili and scallions.

LEMON + HARISSA BABY WEDGES

1 lb 2 oz baby white
  potatoes, quartered
  lengthways

¼ cup neutral oil

zest of 1 lemon and
  juice of ½

2 tsp harissa paste

salt and black
  pepper

Harissa is a North African spice paste that is widely used in stews and marinades, and as a condiment. The peppery and smoky flavor complements these zingy, lemony potato wedges perfectly. Do watch out for super-spicy harissa pastes though – some can really knock ya socks off... unless you're into that.

____

1. Put the potatoes into a saucepan of heavily salted, cold water. Place the pan over a high heat and bring to a boil. Reduce the heat and boil gently for 8–10 minutes, until the potatoes are tender but not falling apart. Drain in a colander. Leave the potatoes in the colander, over the pan on the turned-off stove top, to steam-dry with a dish towel over the top for 5–10 minutes.

2. Meanwhile, heat the oven to 400°F and get the oil into a rimmed baking sheet. Put the sheet into the oven to get the oil hot.

3. Tip the potatoes back into the saucepan and sprinkle over the lemon juice. Add the harissa paste and a pinch of salt and pepper and toss to coat the wedges.

4. Carefully tip the wedges into the baking sheet with the hot oil and put them in the oven for 25 minutes. Give the wedges a shake, then sprinkle over the lemon zest. Return them to the oven for a final 15 minutes, until sticky and golden.

CLASSIC HASH BROWNS

1¼ lbs Yukon Gold
potatoes, peeled
and halved

neutral oil

1 onion, finely
chopped

2 Tbsp cornstarch

herbs and spices
of your choice, to
taste (optional)

salt and black
pepper

flaky sea salt,
to serve

As Dolly Parton once famously said, "Every diet I ever fell off of has been because of a potato." So, when I tumble out of bed and I stumble to the kitchen, I don't reach for the Raisin Bran, I make a big fat hash brown. Be more like Dolly – eat the hash brown.

———

1. Put the potatoes into a saucepan of heavily salted, cold water. Place the pan over a high heat and bring the water to a boil. Reduce the heat and leave the potatoes on a gentle boil for about 20–30 minutes, until they fall off the tip of a knife. Drain in a colander.

2. Once the potatoes are cool enough to handle, divide them into two unequal portions of one third and two thirds. Mash the smaller portion and cut the larger portion into ¼-inch cubes.

3. Heat a large saucepan over a medium heat with a splash of oil. Add the onion and fry for 4 minutes, until soft and translucent. Remove the pan from the heat and add the cubed potatoes and the mashed potatoes. Mix well.

4. Add the cornstarch and season well with salt and pepper. (You can add any other herbs and spices you fancy, let your imagination go wild here.)

5. Line a rimmed baking sheet with parchment paper.

6. Divide your potato mixture into 8 equal portions (about ⅓ cup each) and mold each into a hash-brown shape – I like triangles, but you do you. Place each molded hash brown on your lined baking sheet, as you go. Transfer the baking sheet to the fridge and chill the hash browns for at least 1 hour to firm up.

7. Pour your oil into a deep fryer or a heavy-based saucepan (don't let it come more than halfway up the inside of the pan). Place the pan over a high heat and get the oil to 350°F on a candy thermometer (or use the thermometer in your fryer).

8. In batches, fry the hash browns until golden – about 3 minutes. Drain each batch on paper towel while you fry the remainder. Sprinkle with flaky sea salt to serve.

HASH BROWN BHAJIS

Serves 4

1¾ lbs Yukon Gold potatoes, peeled and coarsely grated

1 onion, peeled and coarsely grated

1 tsp mild curry powder

1 Tbsp cornstarch

½ tsp crushed red pepper flakes

½ tsp nigella seeds, plus optional extra to serve

1 tsp flaky sea salt

neutral oil

black pepper

TO SERVE

coconut-milk yogurt (dairy alternative, not coconut-flavored)

2 Tbsp mango chutney

handful of cilantro, leaves roughly chopped or torn

finely chopped red chili

What could possibly make an onion bhaji better? Potato. Always potato. What else did you expect?! Serve these up as part of a spiced brekky with a poached egg, coconut yogurt and some mango chutney, or as a chunky appetizer.

_____

1. Line a rimmed baking sheet with parchment paper.

2. Tip the grated potato and onion into a clean dish towel. Gather up the edges and squeeze out all of the moisture.

3. Tip the squeezed potato and onion into a mixing bowl and add the curry powder, cornstarch, red pepper flakes, nigella seeds and flaky sea salt and season with pepper. Mix well to evenly combine, then form the mixture into 8 equal patties. Place each patty on the lined baking sheet and transfer them to the fridge for 1 hour to firm up.

4. Heat the oven to 400°F.

5. Meanwhile, heat a large frying pan over medium heat with a large drizzle of oil. In batches of 2 at a time, add the bhajis to the hot oil, frying for 2–4 minutes on each side, until golden-brown all over (this is just to get some color on them). Set aside each batch in a baking sheet while you fry the remainder, topping up the oil and bringing it to temperature as necessary.

6. Transfer the part-cooked bhajis to the oven and bake them for 15–20 minutes, until cooked through.

7. When the bhajis are cooked, spread a few dollops of coconut yogurt on a serving plate, add the spoonfuls of mango chutney, then the top with the bhajis and sprinkle with cilantro and chopped chili. A sprinkling of extra nigella seeds are good over the top, too, if you fancy. Alternatively, just serve the yogurt and chutney in separate bowls for people to dig in themselves, sharing-style.

Live, Laugh, Love, Potato.

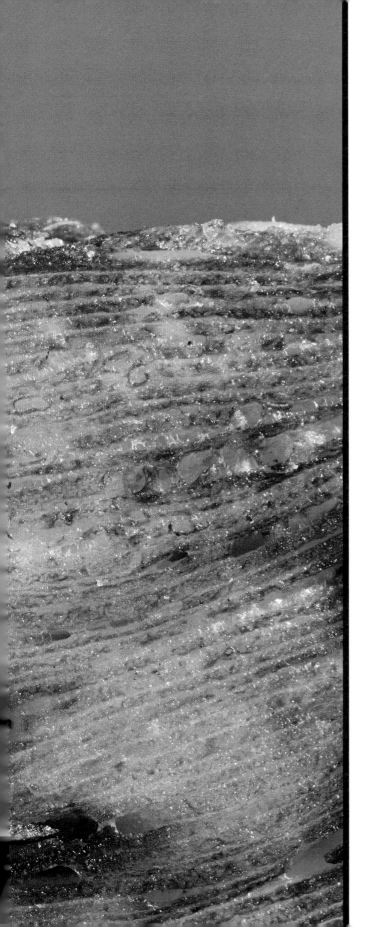

Chapter
Four

15-Hour
Potatoes

THE CLASSIC 15-HOUR POTATOES

3¼ lbs Yukon Gold potatoes, peeled

1⅔ cups heavy cream

1 Tbsp salt, plus extra for sprinkling

neutral oil

This recipe has had hundreds of millions of views and has been recreated across the world. The legend. The icon. The dream. The 15-HOUR POTATO, BABY! Even Goop Queen Gwyneth Paltrow gave it a go. So, don't let the "15-hour" part put you off: 12 hours of that are in the fridge, I'm just dramatic.

This potato dish takes inspiration from the potato pavé developed by US chef Thomas Keller. The 15-hour potato is my version with adapted ingredients and timings to make for the monster that is this delicious potato. Be patient, sit back and enjoy an absolute beauty!

———

1. Thinly slice your potatoes as thin as a potato chip, so almost see-through – using a mandoline is ideal for speed, consistency and ease, but make sure you use a finger guard to avoid any accidents. Put the slices in a bowl.

2. Warm your cream in a saucepan over a medium–high heat and bring to a simmer. Lower the heat and leave simmering until slightly thickened (about 5–10 minutes). Pour this over your slices of potato and mix in the salt.

3. Meanwhile, heat the oven to 275°F.

4. Line a 2-lb loaf pan with parchment paper and layer the spud slices one by one, overlapping them neatly to build a loaf. Place a sheet of parchment paper on top and bake the loaf for 3 hours, until cooked through.

5. Add some weight on top of the cooked, covered loaf. Cans of baked beans are good for this. Transfer it all to the fridge for 12 hours to set. (The waiting is the hardest part.) Then, remove the cans and parchment and turn out the loaf. Trim off each end so that the loaf is perfectly straight, and cut the loaf into 1-inch slices (you'll get about 6 or 7 slices altogether).

6. Pour your oil into a deep fryer or a heavy-based saucepan (don't let it come more than halfway up the inside of the pan). Place the pan over a high heat and get the oil to 375°F on a candy thermometer (or use the thermometer in your fryer). Fry the potato portions in batches for about 1–3 minutes (if you're cutting to my portions), or until golden. Drain each batch on paper towel while you fry the remainder. (You can cut into slabs or squares, just adjust the frying time as necessary.) Once they're all fried, sprinkle with more salt and serve with anything you fancy... although I think these little blocks of deliciousness are good enough to eat as they are.

FAMILY-STYLE 15-HOUR POTATOES

Serves 6

3¼ lbs Yukon Gold potatoes, peeled

1⅔ cups heavy cream

4 garlic cloves, crushed

neutral oil

salt and black pepper

Basically, this is the cheat's way to make the classic 15-hour potato – it doesn't call for precise layering, making it deceptively easy for something that still looks posh, and is ideal when you're cooking for larger groups. Or, for at Christmas if you wanna go all out and impress the in-laws while still looking calm and collected, leaving them wondering... how did he/she/they do it?! Mind you, be prepared to host every year, if you serve up this masterpiece.

———

1. Thinly slice your potatoes as thin as a potato chip, so almost see-through – using a mandoline is ideal for speed, consistency and ease, but make sure you use a finger guard to avoid any accidents. Put the slices in a bowl.

2. Pour your cream into a saucepan and add the garlic. Place the pan over a medium–high heat and bring the cream to a simmer. Lower the heat and leave simmering with the garlic for 5–10 minutes, until slightly thickened. Season well with salt and pepper and tip the potato slices into the pan.

3. Meanwhile, heat the oven to 275°F.

4. Line a 2-lb loaf pan with parchment paper. Tip in the potatoes and cream mixture – the potatoes don't have to be neatly layered on top of one another, but they should be flat. Cover the dish with another sheet of parchment paper, then add a layer of ceramic pie weights to help cement the spuds in place. Bake for 3 hours, until the potatoes are cooked through.

5. Remove the dish from the oven and, with the parchment and pie weights still in place, place the cooked, weighted loaf in the fridge for 12 hours, for the potatoes to set.

6. Once set, remove the pie weights and parchment paper (the pie weights may be a bit greasy, but just give 'em a rinse). Cut the loaf into 1-inch slices (you'll get about 8 slices altogether).

7. Pour your oil into a deep fryer or a heavy-based saucepan (don't let it come more than halfway up the inside of the pan). Place the pan over a high heat and get the oil to 375°F on a candy thermometer (or use the thermometer in your fryer). Fry the potato slices in batches for about 1–3 minutes, or until golden. Drain each batch on paper towel while you fry the remainder. Once they're all fried, season with salt, and dig in.

Serves 6–8

SPICED 15-HOUR POTATOES

3¼ lbs Yukon Gold potatoes, peeled

1⅔ cups heavy cream

4 garlic cloves, finely grated

2 Tbsp mild curry powder

neutral oil

salt and black pepper

If there's one thing we've learnt in this book, it's that potatoes LOVE to take on flavor. Adding curry spice to your 15-hour potato gives it a bit of an edge to really amp up your dinner. I'm all for adding inspired twists to your dishes, so that you can eat it almost every week without ever getting bored. Add a few crushed red pepper flakes, if you really want to get a bit spicy!

——

1. Thinly slice your potatoes as thin as a potato chip, so almost see-through – using a mandoline is ideal for speed, consistency and ease, but make sure you use a finger guard to avoid any accidents. Put the slices in a bowl.

2. Pour your cream into a saucepan and add the garlic and curry powder. Place the pan over a medium–high heat and bring the cream to a simmer. Lower the heat and leave simmering for 5–10 minutes, until thickened. Then, season well with salt and pepper and tip the potato slices into the pan.

3. Heat the oven to 275°F.

4. Line a 2-lb loaf pan with parchment paper and layer the spud slices one by one, overlapping them neatly to build a loaf. Place a sheet of parchment paper on top and bake the loaf for 3 hours, until cooked through.

5. Add some weight on top of the cooked, covered loaf. Cans of baked beans are good for this. Transfer it all to the fridge for 12 hours to set, then remove the cans and parchment and turn out the loaf. Trim off each end so that the loaf is perfectly straight, and cut the loaf into 1-inch slices (you'll get about 6 or 7 slices altogether).

6. Pour your oil into a deep fryer or a heavy-based saucepan (don't let it come more than halfway up the inside of the pan). Place the pan over a high heat and get the oil to 375°F on a candy thermometer (or use the thermometer in your fryer). Fry the potato portions in batches for about 1–3 minutes, or until golden. Drain each batch on paper towel while you fry the remainder. Season with more salt and enjoy!

Serves 6

GOOSE FAT
15-HOUR POTATOES

3¼ lbs Yukon Gold
  potatoes, peeled

⅔ cup goose fat,
  melted

1 Tbsp salt

neutral oil

This is the Mary Poppins of potatoes, because it's practically perfect in every way. If I could find a way to skip that painstaking 12-hour overnight wait, it would be pure perfection, but I can't. No matter – I promise it's worth the wait.

   Using goose fat in this version gives you a festive, fancy spin on the Classic that will cement your status as king or queen of Christmas. It's about time your grandmother with her homemade cookies lost her crown.

――――

1. Thinly slice your potatoes – now, I know I'm getting repetitive, but these are to be so thin that you can nearly see through them and they all have to be the same. If some are thicker, you end up with uneven layers. Using a mandoline is ideal for speed, consistency and ease, but make sure you use a finger guard to avoid any accidents.

2. Heat the oven to 275°F.

3. In a bowl, stir the slices through the melted goose fat and season with the Tbsp of salt.

4. Line a 2-lb loaf pan with parchment paper and layer the spud slices one by one, overlapping them neatly to build a loaf. Place a sheet of parchment paper on top and bake the loaf for 3 hours, until cooked through.

5. Add some weight on top of the cooked, covered loaf. Cans of baked beans are good for this. Transfer it all to the fridge for 12 hours to set, then remove the cans and parchment and turn out the loaf. Trim off each end so that the loaf is perfectly straight, and cut the loaf into 1-inch slices (you'll get about 6 or 7 slices altogether).

6. Pour your oil into a deep fryer or a heavy-based saucepan (don't let it come more than halfway up the inside of the pan). Place the pan over a high heat and get the oil to 350°F on a candy thermometer (or use the thermometer in your fryer). Fry the potato portions in batches for about 1–3 minutes, until golden. Drain each batch on paper towel while you fry the remainder. Sprinkle with more salt and serve with anything you fancy.

CONFIT GARLIC BUTTER 15-HOUR POTATOES

Serves 6

1 cup butter, cubed
  (or if you're not
  clarifying it, use
  ¾ cup plus 2 Tbsp
  ghee instead)

3 whole heads
  of garlic, cloves
  separated and
  peeled

2 rosemary sprigs

3 dried red chilies

3¼ lbs Yukon Gold
  potatoes, peeled

neutral oil

salt and black
  pepper

flaky sea salt,
  to serve

Someone pour butter over me and let me live out my days as a confit garlic 15-hour potato. The confit element gives a mellow, sweet flavor that seeps into the layers of potato. Using garlic this way is honestly magical. If you make this dish, I apologize in advance, because you'll want to eat it every single day.

———

1. First, you need to make some clarified butter (or, if you cba, then get some ghee – it's the same thing, and means you can skip this step). Put your cubes of butter in a rectangular, microwaveable storage dish. Melt the butter in short bursts, then place the dish in the fridge for the clarified butter to set hard. Once set, make a hole in the corner and pour out the buttermilk beneath – use this to marinate chicken or make pancakes. (There's a quicker, but less foolproof alternative method for making clarified butter on page 146, too.)

2. Heat the oven to 275°F

3. Put the garlic cloves, clarified butter, rosemary and chilies in an ovenproof dish. Bake them for 1½ hours. Check the garlic to make sure it's not burning and give it a stir from time to time. If it starts cooking too fast, turn the oven down. Once the cloves are golden and soft, remove the rosemary and chilies and, using a stick blender, mush up the garlic until smooth. Set aside – but don't let it set, keep it warm-ish.

4. Using a mandoline, thinly slice your potatoes so that they're almost see-through (use the finger guard). Tip them into a large bowl, then mix them really well with your blended garlic-and-butter situation, and season with salt and pepper.

5. Line a 2-lb loaf pan with parchment paper and layer the spud slices one by one, overlapping them neatly to build a loaf. Place a sheet of parchment paper on top and bake the loaf for 3 hours, until cooked through.

6. Add some weight on top of the cooked, covered loaf. Cans of baked beans are good for this. Transfer it all to the fridge for 12 hours to set, then remove the cans and parchment and turn out the loaf. Trim off each end to straighten, and cut the loaf into 1-inch slices (you'll get about 6 or 7 slices altogether).

7. Pour your oil into a deep fryer or a heavy-based saucepan (don't let it come more than halfway up the inside of the pan). Place the pan over a high heat and get the oil to 375°F on a candy thermometer (or use the thermometer in your fryer). Fry the potato slices in batches for 1–3 minutes, or until golden. Drain each batch on paper towel while you fry the remainder. Sprinkle with flaky salt and serve as you fancy... for me, this one is good as it is.

Serves 6

BACON 15-HOUR POTATOES

3¼ lbs Yukon Gold
potatoes, peeled

1 cup duck fat, beef
tallow or ghee

4 garlic cloves,
peeled

2 thyme sprigs

12 slices of smoked
bacon

neutral oil

Unless you're a vegetarian, it has to be said that everything gets better with bacon. Every single dish in this book could just have a "with bacon" variation, because it marries with cheese, with cream and with garlic so well. Maybe that could be the next book: Potato + Bacon. I love it.

_____

1. Thinly slice your potatoes so that they are almost see-through – using a mandoline is ideal for speed, consistency and ease, but make sure you use a finger guard to avoid any accidents. Put the slices in a bowl.

2. Gently melt the duck fat or beef tallow in a saucepan with the garlic cloves and all the thyme. Meanwhile, heat the oven to 275°F.

3. Remove the garlic and herbs from the melted fat and pour it over the potatoes in the bowl.

4. Line a 2-lb loaf pan with parchment paper and start layering the spud slices one by one, always neatly overlapping. After every 4 layers of potato, lay down strips of bacon to completely cover the potato layer beneath. Then, repeat with another 4 layers of the potatoes, then a layer of bacon, and so on until there are no more slices left, finishing with a layer of potatoes.

5. Cover the top with parchment paper and pour over pie weights to weigh down the loaf. Transfer the loaf to the oven and bake for 3 hours, until cooked through. Move it all to the fridge for 12 hours, until the loaf is set.

6. Once set, remove the pie weights and parchment paper (the pie weights may be a bit greasy, but just give 'em a rinse). Turn out your potato loaf and trim off each end so that the loaf is perfectly straight. Cut the loaf into 1-inch slices (you'll get about 6 or 7 slices altogether; you can cut each slice again, into smaller chunks, if you like – just watch the frying time in the next step).

7. Pour your oil into a deep fryer or a heavy-based saucepan (don't let it come more than halfway up the inside of the pan). Place the pan over a high heat and get the oil to 375°F on a candy thermometer (or use the thermometer in your fryer). Fry the potato portions in batches for 1–3 minutes, or until golden. Drain each batch on paper towel while you fry the remainder. Serve them up and enjoy that bacony goodness.

Serves 6

ROOT VEG 15-HOUR POTATOES

¾ cup plus 1 Tbsp
goose fat or
clarified butter
(see page 146)

1 Tbsp flaky sea salt,
plus extra to serve

4 garlic cloves,
minced

2 thyme sprigs

2¼ lbs Yukon Gold
potatoes, peeled

½ rutabaga, peeled

¼ celery root, peeled

½ butternut squash
(the non-seedy,
straight bit), peeled

neutral oil

salt and black
pepper

Some people say I don't cook enough healthy food. So, you know what? I'm throwing all the veggies into the mix here. This baby counts as three of my five-a-day, doesn't it? Please? No longer will rutabaga, celery root and squash languish at the bottom of a stew. They are now the talk of the town in this golden, buttery, CROUNCHY delight.

_____

1. Melt the goose fat or clarified butter in a large saucepan and add in the flaky salt, garlic and thyme to infuse on the heat while you slice your potatoes.

2. Get your potatoes and slice them as thin as a potato chip, so almost see-through – using a mandoline is ideal for speed, consistency and ease, but use a finger guard to avoid any accidents. Put the slices in a large bowl. Repeat for the rutabaga, celery root and butternut squash, putting those slices each into a separate bowl, ready for individual layering.

3. Heat the oven to 275°F.

4. Remove the garlic and herbs from the infused fat and pour half of it over the potatoes. Divide the other half equally between the sliced vegetables. Season well with salt and pepper.

5. Line a 2-lb loaf pan with parchment paper and start to layer up the potatoes, neatly one by one, always overlapping. After every 4 layers of potato, add individual layers of squash, celery root and rutabaga to completely cover the layer below, then repeat – potatoes, veg, potatoes, veg, until everything is used up.

6. Place a piece of parchment paper on top of the final layer, then weigh it all down with pie weights. Bake the loaf for 3 hours, then remove it from the oven and refrigerate overnight with the weights still on top.

7. Remove the weights and parchment paper and turn out the loaf. Trim the ends to neaten them up, and cut the loaf into 1-inch slices (you'll get about 6 or 7 slices altogether).

8. Pour your oil into a deep fryer or a heavy-based saucepan (don't let it come more than halfway up the inside of the pan). Place the pan over a high heat and get the oil to 375°F on a candy thermometer (or use the thermometer in your fryer). Fry the potato portions in batches for 1–3 minutes, or until golden brown and crispy. Drain each batch on paper towel while you fry the remainder. Season with flaky sea salt and serve up.

THE VEGAN RED THAI 15-HOUR POTATOES

Serves 6

2 x 13.5-oz cans of full-fat coconut milk

2 Tbsp good-quality store-bought red Thai curry paste

3¼ lbs Yukon Gold potatoes, peeled

neutral oil

flaky sea salt

It's finally here – the Vegan 15-hour Potato. Generally, the 15-hour potato needs the fat to hold it together, so it took a bit of thought to remove that and still get a vegan option to work and taste delicious. Enter coconut milk and red Thai curry paste. And when I tell you that this dish is ABSOLUTELY delicious, I'm thinking that this needs to stand alone as a vegan main dish. So good!

––––

1. Pour the coconut milk into a large saucepan and place it over a medium–low heat. Leave the coconut milk to reduce by half – this takes about 45 minutes to 1 hour, but it's worth it. Whisk the Thai curry paste into the thickened milk.

2. Heat the oven to 275°F.

3. Thinly slice your potatoes as thin as a potato chip, so almost see-through – using a mandoline is ideal for speed, consistency and ease, but make sure you use a finger guard to avoid any accidents. Put the slices in a large bowl.

4. Pour over the coconut milk mixture, add a big pinch of flaky sea salt and toss the potatoes to coat.

5. Line a 2-lb loaf pan with parchment paper and layer the spud slices one by one, overlapping them neatly to build a loaf. Place a piece of parchment paper on top of the final layer, then weigh it all down with pie weights. Bake the loaf for 3 hours, then remove it from the oven and refrigerate overnight with the pie weights still on top.

6. Remove the pie weights and parchment paper and turn out the loaf. Trim off each end to straighten, and cut the loaf into 1-inch slices (you'll get about 6 or 7 slices altogether).

7. Pour your oil into a deep fryer or a heavy-based saucepan (don't let it come more than halfway up the inside of the pan). Place the pan over a high heat and get the oil to 375°F on a candy thermometer (or use the thermometer in your fryer). Fry the potato portions in batches for 1–3 minutes, or until golden. Drain each batch on paper towel while you fry the remainder. Sprinkle with flaky sea salt and serve with anything you fancy... for me, this one is good enough on its own! Dig in!

Serves 7

CHICKEN FAT
15-HOUR POTATOES

⅔ cup chicken fat/
schmaltz

2 rosemary sprigs

2 thyme sprigs

3¼ lbs Yukon Gold
potatoes, peeled

1 Tbsp salt

neutral oil

flaky salt, to serve

Adding chicken fat to your 15-hour potatoes gives your potato stacks a deeply savory flavor and an insanely crunchy crust that honestly can't be topped.

———

1. Melt the chicken fat/schmaltz in a large saucepan and add in the rosemary and thyme to infuse while you slice your potatoes.

2. Get your potatoes and slice them as thin as a potato chip, so almost see-through – using a mandoline is ideal for speed, consistency and ease, but make sure you use a finger guard to avoid any accidents. Put the slices in a large bowl.

3. Remove the herbs from the infused chicken fat and pour the fat over the potatoes in the bowl. Add the Tbsp of salt and toss the potatoes to coat.

4. Line a 2-lb loaf pan with parchment paper and layer the spud slices one by one, overlapping them neatly to build a loaf. Place a sheet of parchment paper on top and bake the loaf for 3 hours, until cooked through.

5. Add some weight on top of the cooked, covered loaf. Cans of baked beans are good for this. Transfer it all to the fridge for 12 hours to set, then remove the cans and parchment and turn out the loaf. Trim off each end so that the loaf is perfectly straight, and cut the loaf into 1-inch slices (you'll get about 6 or 7 slices altogether). This version is particularly delicious as cubes or columns, so go for it if you like and just keep an eye on the frying time in the next step.

6. Pour your oil into a deep fryer or a heavy-based saucepan (don't let it come more than halfway up the inside of the pan). Place the pan over a high heat and get the oil to 350°F on a candy thermometer (or use the thermometer in your fryer). Fry the potato portions in batches for about 1–3 minutes, until golden. Drain each batch on paper towel while you fry the remainder. Season with flaky sea salt, and serve up!

Chapter
Five

World
Classics

POMMES ANNA

Serves 4–8

2 lbs russet
  potatoes, peeled

5 Tbsp butter, plus
  extra if needed

olive oil

salt and black
  pepper

No one quite knows which French beauty this dish was named after, so shout-out to the mysterious Anna who gave us this goddess among potatoes. You need a bit of technical skill for it, but I once made it live on TV, under the spotlights with intense questioning and a faulty oven... so that was fun!

———

1. Using a mandoline (with the finger guard) or by hand with a knife, slice your potatoes to around 1/16 inch thick – try to keep the slices as even as possible. Place them in a bowl of cold water as you go, so they don't start to brown.

2. Melt about one generous Tbsp of your butter with a splash of olive oil in an ovenproof 8-inch frying pan over a medium heat.

3. Use a 1-inch round cookie cutter to cut rounds from the potato slices, otherwise just leave them as they are. Make a layer of potatoes in a neat spiral in one even layer, starting at the center and working your way round to the edge, making sure you overlap the potatoes so they stick together when cooking. Once you have completed the first layer, season with salt and pepper and dot with a few small pieces of the remaining butter. Continue layering like this until you've used all your potato slices, following the spiral shape without any gaps (gaps mean the layers won't stick together properly). Remember to add salt, pepper and butter between each layer.

4. Cover the potatoes in the frying pan with a circle of parchment paper and place a small plate on top to weigh the slices down and help everything stick together. Leave it over a medium heat for around 20–25 minutes, keeping an eye on it so that it doesn't burn. Remove the plate occasionally to check it's not browning too quickly at the edges. After the first 10–12 minutes, when the slices have stuck together, use a flat metal spatula to very gently lift up the edge of the potato spiral to have a bit more of a look underneath. If it is going a little bit dark, turn down the heat for a few minutes.

5. Meanwhile, heat the oven to 400°F.

6. Once you can see the edges turn golden brown and crispy and the top of the potatoes have softened, remove the plate and parchment paper and transfer the frying pan to the oven to brown the top – just 10 minutes or so.

7. Put a dish towel underneath your frying pan. Place a serving plate or board on top – you want it to fit tightly to the top of your pan to keep all of the remaining butter and oil inside when you flip. Then, use the dish towel to protect your hands while you press the pan and serving dish together and do a quick flip so the pommes Anna inverts on to the plate without sliding around too much. Remove the pan (use your dish towel as the handle will be very hot!) and serve.

ALIGOT

1½ lbs Yukon Gold potatoes, peeled and cut into ¾-inch rounds

⅔–1 cup heavy cream

3 Tbsp butter

12 oz fresh mozzarella (drained weight)

¾ cup shredded extra-sharp cheddar

¾ cup shredded comté or gruyère

¾ cup shredded taleggio

salt and black pepper

Like pommes Anna (see page 118), this recipe comes from France. Officially, the authentic cheese to use is tomme fraîche (a compacted curd cheese) – but the French seem to like to keep all the supplies to themselves. There are some American artisanal dairies that are producing similar cheeses, but if you can't find anything then this is my more attainable take on the French classic and it's still beautiful. You can, of course, adapt the cheeses to your taste, but I love the nuttiness the comté brings. Don't hate me, France!

––––

1. Put the potato slices into a saucepan of heavily salted, cold water and bring to a boil. Reduce the heat and leave on a gentle boil for around 20 minutes, until the potatoes fall off the tip of a knife. Drain in a colander.

2. Put the colander back on the empty pan on the turned-off stove top, cover the potatoes with a clean dish towel and leave them to steam-dry for 5–10 minutes (see page 16).

3. Portion by portion, pass the steam-dried potatoes through a strainer or potato ricer into a saucepan, or mash them with a potato masher.

4. In a microwave-safe pitcher or bowl, add ⅔ cup of the heavy cream, along with the butter. Tear in one-third of the mozzarella, then microwave on high for around 45–60 seconds, until the cheese has melted (or you can do this in a saucepan over a medium heat, stirring constantly). Pour this into the potatoes and, using a rubber spatula, mix well. Stir through the rest of the cheeses, tearing up the remaining mozzarella as you go.

5. Place the saucepan back over a low heat and keep mixing until everything is fully incorporated – this can take some time, but just keep going until all the cheeses have melted and combined. The consistency should be like cheese fondue so add more warmed cream, depending on how it's going, if you need.

TARTIFLETTE

6 slices of thick-cut
  smoked bacon,
  diced

1 lb 2 oz fingerling
  potatoes, scrubbed
  and cut into ½-inch
  cubes

1 onion, diced

3 garlic cloves,
  chopped

about 2 cups
  vegetable or
  chicken broth

generous ¾ cup
  heavy cream

7 oz Delice du Jura
  or brie

salt and black
  pepper

One of my all-time favorite French potato dishes, tartiflette originates from the Alps and is popular during après-ski. Not that I've experienced skiing, après-ski or even explored the Alps for that matter, but a girl can dream. I'll just cook myself a big pan of these beauties and imagine I'm there. Reblochon is the traditional cheese but difficult to find in the US, so I've suggested some alternatives here.

———

1. Tip the bacon into a medium, ovenproof frying pan and get it over a medium–high heat. Fry for about 8–10 minutes, until crispy and caramelized. Remove from the pan (but leave the fat behind).

2. Add the potatoes and onion to the pan and fry for 10 minutes, until there is a little color on them. Add your garlic, season with salt and pepper, and return the bacon to the pan.

3. Pour in your broth to just cover the potatoes, bring to a boil and leave to boil until all the liquid has gone. Test the tenderness of the spuds – if they need longer, add in a splash of water and repeat the process.

4. Heat the oven to 400°F.

5. Once the potatoes are tender, turn the heat down a little and pour over your cream. Cook the cream until it has thickened and is almost coating the spuds. Take the pan off the heat and slice up your cheese.

6. Layer the gooey cheese over the potato mixture and place it in the oven for 10 minutes, until completely melted. Turn the oven to the broil setting and leave it on high to get some color on top.

7. Once the cheese is golden and bubbling, carefully remove the pan from the broiler. Remember – the handle will be hot. Serve the tartiflette straight away with crusty bread.

DAUPHINOISE

2¾ lbs Yukon Gold potatoes, peeled

2½ cups heavy cream

3 garlic cloves, peeled

pinch of white pepper

pinch of ground nutmeg

salt

I really should have named this chapter "French potatoes I'm obsessed with" because the French can do no wrong when it comes to a spud. This dauphinoise is a classic and, like Brigitte Bardot, will become the main attraction and star of the show. And the classic version has NO cheese!

———

1. Find an ovenproof dish that fits your whole potatoes snugly inside – this will give you the right size for your finished dauphinoise.

2. Slice your potatoes ¼-inch thick, dropping the slices into water as you go, so that they don't go brown. Heat the oven to 350°F.

3. Put the cream and garlic in a large saucepan and season with some salt, and the pepper and nutmeg. Place the pan over a medium–high heat. Leave the cream to warm until thickened slightly (about 5–10 minutes). Then, take the pan off the heat.

4. Now, there are two ways to get your potatoes into the dish. You can drain them and add them to the cream, then just pour this mixture into your baking dish and bake them. Or, you can be obsessive like me and layer them neatly. If you are layering them and also want to turn them out and slice the dauphinoise into individual portions, then you will need to line your dish with parchment paper. Then, layer the potatoes, just slightly overlapping. In between the potato layers, season with salt and add a little of the cream. Once all the potatoes are used up, pour over the remaining cream.

5. Whichever method you use, cover the top of the dish with parchment paper and bake for 40 minutes, then remove the parchment and return the dish to the oven for another 20–30 minutes, until the dauphinoise is golden on top.

6. Once cooked, you can eat the potatoes straight away, or you can add a weight on top like I did. You'll need to lay a piece of parchment paper over the potatoes, then top that with another baking dish or pan – one that fits just inside the potato dish. Weigh that down with cans of your choice or with ceramic pie weights, and leave the dauphinoise to cool.

7. Once the potatoes are cold, refrigerate for 30 minutes to 1 hour, or overnight if you're patient enough. Then, remove the weight and parchment paper, cut the dauphinoise into portions and reheat in the oven at 350°F for 15 minutes, until piping hot.

BATATA HARRA

14 oz Yukon Gold
  potatoes, cut into
  ¾-inch cubes
  (skin on)

neutral oil

drizzle of olive oil

2 garlic cloves,
  chopped

1 tsp crushed red
  pepper flakes

small bunch of
  cilantro, leaves
  chopped

juice of 1 lemon,
  to taste

salt and black
  pepper

I first made this dish during my "Around The World In 80 Potatoes" series and fell in love. A spicy Lebanese recipe consisting of fragrant, crispy cubes, it is perfect to zhuzh up your breakfast with a lil' Middle Eastern flair (who can wait all day to enjoy the potatoes for supper?). If you're like me, massively whack up the heat and deal with the consequences later.

———

1. Place the potato cubes in a saucepan of heavily salted, cold water and bring to a boil. Reduce the heat and gently boil until the cubes are starting to go tender (around 10 minutes), then drain in a colander. Leave the potatoes to steam-dry in the colander set over the pan on the turned-off stove top for 10 minutes.

2. Pour your neutral oil into a deep fryer or a heavy-based saucepan (don't let it come more than halfway up the inside of the pan). Place the pan over a high heat and get the oil to 350°F on a candy thermometer (or use the thermometer in your fryer). Fry the steam-dried potato cubes in batches for about 6–8 minutes, until golden. Drain each batch on paper towel while you fry the remainder.

3. Add the drizzle of olive oil to a large frying pan over a medium–high heat. When hot, add the garlic and red pepper flakes and fry for 1–2 minutes, until fragrant. Add the chopped cilantro, and the lemon juice to taste. Season well with salt and pepper, then toss through the crispy potato cubes and serve immediately.

BRATKARTOFFELN

Serves 4

1¾ lbs russet
potatoes, peeled

7 oz thick-cut
smoked bacon,
diced

1 onion, finely
chopped

neutral oil

1 generous Tbsp
butter

2 garlic cloves,
crushed or finely
grated

salt and black
pepper

My idol and absolute queen, Nigella Lawson, recommended I make bratkartoffeln for the letter B in my "A–Z of Potatoes" series. How could I refuse? She once called me the "High Priestess of Potatoes" and I am still fan-girling over this three years later. I will 100-per-cent be having that engraved on my headstone. (P.S. She was right to recommend it, because this German specialty is bloomin' lovely.)

————

1. Get your whole potatoes into a saucepan of heavily salted, cold water. Place the pan over a high heat, bring the water to a boil, then reduce the heat and leave at a gentle boil for 15–20 minutes, until the potatoes fall off the tip of a knife. Drain in a colander.

2. Meanwhile, tip the bacon into a large, cold frying pan. Place it over a high heat so that the fat from the bacon gets golden and delicious. Keep an eye on it and stir occasionally. Once the bacon is golden, tip it out of the pan and reserve for later.

3. Reduce the temperature under the frying pan and add the onion. Drizzle with oil, season with salt and pepper, then fry for 8–10 minutes, until golden and soft. Tip the onion out of the pan and reserve it for later.

4. Leave the drained potatoes to cool just enough so that you can handle them (or put on some gloves and get to work). We are going to slice the spuds into even rounds, about ¼ inch thick.

5. Get the frying pan back over a medium heat. Add the butter and another drizzle of oil and, once the butter is bubbly, add the potato rounds. Depending on the size of your pan, you may have to cook the spuds in batches. You want to be able to lay each slice of potato flat on the bottom of the pan; the slices shouldn't stack on top of one another.

6. Once the potato slices are brown on one side (about 3 minutes), flip them over and do the same to the other side. Season each batch well with salt and pepper, then set the slices aside on a plate while you fry the remainder. Repeat, adding oil as needed, until all the potatoes are golden on both sides.

7. Tip all the fried potatoes back into the pan together (still over medium heat) and add the garlic. Cook for a couple of minutes. Then, add the bacon and onion back to the pan and mix well. It should only take a couple of minutes for the bacon and onion to warm back up, then you are ready to serve.

POUTINE

1¾ lbs long, fat
   mealy potatoes
   (preferably russet),
   peeled and sliced
   into fries about
   the size of your
   index finger

¼ cup neutral oil

1¼ cups chicken
   broth

1¼ cups beef broth

2 garlic cloves,
   bashed but left
   whole

2 thyme sprigs

2 rosemary sprigs

3 Tbsp cornstarch

2 Tbsp butter, cubed

7 oz fresh mozzarella
   (or cheese curds, if
   you can find them)

salt

If my research is right, *poutine* means "hot mess"... I've never related to a potato dish more. I am the poutine of the cheffing world. I love it. You've got golden fries (I'm using my oven fries, but feel free to use classic fries) topped with squeaky cheese curds and doused in thick, velvety brown gravy. Basically, it's an upgrade on that classic post-night-out order from your local takeout spot. My kinda meal. In 2023, I was lucky enough to be in Montreal, Canada, where this dish comes from. Authentic poutine is incredible.

—————

1. Heat the oven to 425°F.

2. Place your cut potatoes in a bowl of cold water to soak for 2–3 minutes, then rinse to remove any excess starch. Tip them into a large saucepan of heavily salted, cold water (make sure they are covered). Bring the water to a boil, then reduce to a simmer and cook for a further 7–10 minutes, until the potatoes are tender but not falling apart. Drain in a colander.

3. One by one, spread the potatoes out over a rack placed over a baking sheet (be careful so as not to break them up). Place a dish towel over them and leave them to steam-dry for 5–10 minutes.

4. Meanwhile, add the oil to a large rimmed baking sheet and place it in the oven to heat up for 5–10 minutes, or until hot.

5. Carefully remove the baking sheet from the oven and tip the potatoes into the hot oil, giving them one little mix so they get coated – the oil should be hot enough that it sizzles when you add the dry potatoes. Return the baking sheet to the oven for 45 minutes, turning the fries over halfway through cooking, until they are golden and crispy all over.

6. While the fries are cooking, make your gravy. Add both broths, and the garlic, thyme and rosemary to a saucepan and bring to a boil, then reduce the liquid by half (about 5 minutes). In a separate small bowl, mix the cornstarch with 2 Tbsp of water.

7. Discard the garlic and herbs from the pan, then turn down the heat on the reduced broth and whisk in the cornstarch slurry and the cubes of butter to thicken. Taste and adjust the seasoning, if necessary.

8. To serve, stack your fries high, tear up your mozzarella (for cheese curds, leave them as they are) and scatter this on top. Pour over your hot, thick gravy. Dig in.

LATKES

Makes 6–8

1¼ lbs russet
  potatoes, grated
  (skin on)

1 onion, grated

1 large egg

sprinkle of panko
  breadcrumbs
  or flour

neutral oil

salt and black
  pepper

applesauce and sour
  cream, to serve

This is a Jewish dish often served with applesauce or sour cream. If a combo of apples and potatoes doesn't sound that great to you, remember the French call potatoes *pommes de terre*, which is the apples of the earth. So basically, they're not that different.

——

1. Squeeze the grated potato through a clean non-terry dish towel or cheesecloth, keeping the drained potato water in a large bowl. Squeeze out the onion, too (in this case, you can discard any squeezed juice).

2. Leave the potato water to sit for a while (about 3 minutes should do it), then carefully pour away the water part and keep the potato starch that is left at the bottom of the bowl.

3. Put your potatoes and onion into the bowl with the potato starch and mix. Crack in the egg, season with salt and pepper and sprinkle in the breadcrumbs or flour – you want to make a clumpy dough, so use just enough to help bind the mixture together. Mix well and leave to rest for 10 minutes.

4. Pour about a ½-inch depth of oil into a deep frying pan. Place the pan over a medium–high heat and let the oil get hot – it's hot enough when a little bit of your potato mixture dropped in makes that beautiful sizzling sound.

5. Take about a tablespoonful of potato mixture and squeeze and shape it into a thin patty in your hands. Add it to the hot oil and fry until golden and crispy – about 2 minutes on each side, so that you get nice, brown crispy bits around the edges. Remove the cooked patty to a plate lined with paper towel and keep warm. Repeat, frying the patties in batches and making sure the oil doesn't lose temperature until you've finished all the mixture. You should get about 8 patties altogether.

6. Serve with applesauce and sour cream.

POMMES DAUPHINE

12 oz Yukon Gold
 potatoes, peeled
 and sliced into
 ¾-inch rounds

3 Tbsp whole milk

3 Tbsp butter

½ cup all-purpose
 flour

2 eggs

neutral oil

salt and black
 pepper

FOR THE FILLING

⅓ cup crème fraîche

handful of chopped
 dill, plus extra to
 garnish

juice of ½ lime

pinch of ground
 ginger

These crispy, crunchy potato puffs are a perfect mix of choux pastry and mashed potatoes. The beauty of this dish is that you can use whatever filling you want. I opted for crème fraîche, dill and ginger, but you could go for a cheesy béchamel sauce, sour cream and something else saucy and delicious. The choice is yours.

———

1. Put the potato slices into a saucepan of heavily salted, cold water. Bring the water to a boil, then lower the heat and simmer the potatoes for about 20 minutes, until they fall off the tip of a knife. Drain in a colander. Put the colander back on the empty pan on the turned-off stove top, cover the potatoes with a clean dish towel and leave them to steam-dry for 5–10 minutes (see page 16).

2. Portion by portion, pass the steam-dried potatoes through a strainer or potato ricer into a bowl, or mash them with a potato masher – you should have about 1¼ cups of mash (if you've used a potato ricer or strainer then give the mashed potatoes a good stir before measuring them so that they are not so fluffy). Keep warm.

3. Pour the milk into a saucepan with 3 Tbsp of water. Add the butter and place the pan over a high heat until the butter has completely melted and the mixture is bubbling (about 4 minutes). Then, turn the heat down to medium and add the flour, mixing constantly until a dough forms and it's completely cooked and not sticking to the pan. Remove the pan from the heat and, one by one, beat in your eggs. Keep beating until the mixture has cooled and the dough is gorgeously smooth. Add the 1¼ cups of mash and beat until fully combined.

4. Pour your oil into a deep fryer or a heavy-based saucepan (don't let it come more than halfway up the inside of the pan). Place the pan over a high heat and get the oil to 350°F on a candy thermometer (or use the thermometer in your fryer). In batches, roll the potato dough into a ping-pong-sized balls between your palms, then add them to the hot oil (about 3 or 4 balls at a time, depending on the size of your pan). Fry for about 2 minutes, until golden and crispy. Drain each batch on paper towel while you fry the remainder. Season with salt and set aside to cool slightly.

5. Combine all the filling ingredients in a bowl and season with salt and pepper to taste. If you have a small, squeezy bottle, spoon the mixture into it, otherwise you can use a piping bag fitted with a small, plain tip.

6. When the dauphines have cooled slightly, make a hole in the bottom of each ball with your bottle or piping tip and squeeze or pipe in some of that delicious filling. Then, serve with a perfect squeeze of the filing on top and garnished with a little piece of dill. Very fancy and perfect as a pre-dinner canapé or appetizer.

RÖSTI

Serves 6–8

2¾–4¼ lbs Yukon
 Gold potatoes,
 peeled and grated

1 large onion, grated

1 heaping tsp
 crushed red pepper
 flakes

2 Tbsp clarified
 butter (see page 146)
 or ghee, melted

salt and black
 pepper

TO SERVE

4 tsp crème fraîche
 or sour cream

1 Tbsp caviar

flaky sea salt

chopped chives
 and picked dill,
 to garnish

Not only have the Swiss introduced us to the rösti, but those lovely people have also delighted us with fancy AF chocolate, some pretty decent Alps and the dreamy cheese fondue. I'll need manually rolling back down one of their mountains, if I ever get the chance to visit.

____

1. Put the grated potato and onion together into a clean non-terry dish towel and squeeze out all of the liquid.

2. Put the dried potato and onion into a mixing bowl with the red pepper flakes and melted clarified butter or ghee. Stir to combine, then season well with salt and pepper.

3. Place a non-stick medium frying pan (about 9 inches diameter) over a medium heat. Once it's hot, fully fill the pan with a thick layer of potato mixture. Don't press the potato too much into the pan, you still need there to be little air pockets so that the steam can cook the rösti all the way through (if it's too compressed it won't cook in the center). Leave to cook for 15–20 minutes, not turning up the heat too high – think low and slow. You can tell when the edges start to go translucent/slightly brown that the rösti is ready to flip.

4. To do this, I recommend placing a cutting board or large plate on top of the frying pan, inverting it so that the rösti lands on the board or plate, then carefully sliding the rösti back into the frying pan, uncooked side down, to continue. Cook for another 10 minutes, until golden and crisp on the underside and cooked all the way through.

5. Transfer the rösti to a cutting board and slice it into wedges. Put a blob of crème fraîche on each slice, top with a few pieces of caviar and sprinkle over some flaky sea salt, chives and dill, to finish. Not just fancy – totally posh!

In the Words of Dolly Parton...

I've Never Met a Spud I Didn't Like.

CROQUETTES

1¾ lbs Yukon gold
  potatoes

3 oz uncooked
  chorizo sausage,
  diced or crumbled

¾ cup crumbled
  goat cheese

1 Tbsp cornstarch

1 egg, beaten

2 cups panko
  breadcrumbs

2 Tbsp all-purpose
  flour

salt and black
  pepper

aïoli, to garnish
  (optional)

The gorgeous breaded and fried coating on croquettes keeps that gooey loveliness locked in and is the perfect snack or starter. Pleeeease be aware of how chuffin' hot these are when first served – I burn myself EVERY. SINGLE. TIME. But, then, that's because I have absolutely no patience and want the satisfaction of getting that molten cheese straight in my mouth before anyone else gets a look in.

———

1. Heat the oven to 425°F. Prick the potatoes all over with a fork and bake them straight on the rack for 50–60 minutes, until tender on the inside.

2. Slice the potatoes in half and scoop out the flesh. Push the flesh through a fine strainer or potato ricer to get a fine, dry mash. Set aside to cool. (You can use the skins for any of the recipes on pages 176–86, if you like.)

3. Heat a dry frying pan over a medium heat. Add the chorizo and fry for 7–10 minutes, until the pieces have released their oil and crisped up. Drain off the oil and add the chorizo to the mashed potatoes. Add the goat cheese and cornstarch, and season with salt and pepper, then mix everything together to form a dough. Divide the dough into 12 equal pieces (about 3 Tbsp each) and shape each into a ball (about the size of a ping-pong ball) or cylinder, transferring them to a baking sheet lined with parchment paper as you go.

4. Refrigerate the balls or cylinders for at least 1 hour (or ideally overnight) to firm up.

5. Whisk the egg in a bowl, then tip the breadcrumbs into another bowl, and the flour into a third.

6. Season your flour well with salt and pepper. One by one, toss each chilled potato ball or cylinder carefully through the flour, then coat it in the egg, then in the breadcrumbs.

7. Pour your oil into a deep fryer or a heavy-based saucepan (don't let it come more than halfway up the inside of the pan). Place the pan over a high heat and get the oil to 350°F on a candy thermometer (or use the thermometer in your fryer). Fry the croquettes in batches, until golden brown and crispy – about 4–5 minutes per batch. Drain each batch on paper towel while you fry the remainder. Garnish with aïoli, if you like, and sprinkle with salt to serve.

PATATAS BRAVAS

1¼ lbs Yukon Gold
  potatoes, peeled
  and cut into
  ¾-inch cubes

¼ cup neutral oil

2 Tbsp olive oil

1 red onion, finely
  diced

2 garlic cloves,
  minced or finely
  grated

1 Tbsp tomato paste

2 tsp smoked
  paprika

½ tsp chili powder

1 tsp Italian
  seasoning

1 x 14-oz can of diced
  tomatoes

pinch of granulated
  sugar, if needed

salt and black
  pepper

aïoli, to serve

chopped Italian
  parsley leaves or
  cilantro, to serve

If you need me, you can find me sunbathing with a sangria or Fanta Limón in one hand and a bowl of spiced patatas bravas in the other. When I was a child, my mom and I would holiday in Spain every year, so this recipe has a special place in my heart. Indulge in this Spanish specialty, then go book a flight. Shout-out to anyone else who would also holiday near regions like Málaga, Benalmádena, Fuengirola or Mijas as kid. What a place!

———

1. Put the potatoes into a saucepan of heavily salted, cold water. Place the pan over a high heat and bring the water to a boil. Reduce the heat and leave on a gentle boil for about 7–10 minutes, until the potatoes fall off the tip of a knife. Drain in a colander, place the colander back over the pan on the turned-off stove top and leave the potato cubes to steam-dry for 10–15 minutes, until they become white around the edges – this gives the fluffiness!

2. Heat the oven to 400°F. Pour the neutral oil into a rimmed baking sheet and place that in the oven to heat up.

3. Carefully tip the cubed potatoes into the hot oil in the baking sheet and toss to coat. Roast in the oven for 45–50 minutes, turning halfway through, until golden brown all over. (Alternatively, you can deep-fry the cubes in a saucepan half-filled with neutral oil at 350°F for about 3 minutes, until they are golden and crispy all over.)

4. Meanwhile, heat the olive oil in a frying pan over a medium heat. Add the onion and fry for 5–6 minutes, until softened. Add the garlic, tomato paste, smoked paprika, chili powder and Italian seasoning and stir to combine. Cook out the tomato paste for a few minutes, then add the canned tomatoes and season well with salt and pepper. Leave the sauce to reduce for 20–25 minutes, until thickened and rich, then taste for seasoning and add a pinch of sugar to balance, if needed. Keep the sauce warm while the potatoes finish roasting.

5. Tip the potatoes into a serving bowl, then either stir through the tomato sauce or pour the sauce over the top. Then drizzle with aïoli and sprinkle with the chopped herbs, to serve.

HONEY + CHILI NOISETTES

4 Yukon Gold
  potatoes, peeled

3 Tbsp butter

2 garlic cloves, thinly
  sliced

1 tsp crushed red
  pepper flakes

2 tsp honey

flaky sea salt,
  to serve

Noisette is French for "hazelnut" and basically refers to the way we cut and cook the potatoes in this dish – into hazelnut shapes that are coated in browned butter to give a fragrant nuttiness. They are also known as "fried potato balls", but that just doesn't sound as cute, to be honest. I personally like to describe them as golden nuggets because they really start to glisten once frying in that glorious butter.

———

1. Using a 1-inch melon baller, cut balls from your potatoes. You should get about 5 balls per potato.

2. Get your balls in a saucepan of heavily salted, cold water. Place the pan over a high heat, bring the water to a boil, then lower the heat and gently boil the balls for about 5–7 minutes, until falling off the tip of a knife. Don't let them get too soft as you don't want them to lose their shape and go mushy. Drain the balls in a colander and leave to steam-dry for 5–10 minutes.

3. Place a frying pan over a medium heat and add the butter. Once it has melted and turned frothy, add the potato balls and cook for 10–15 minutes, stirring to turn the potatoes throughout, until the butter has turned brown. Add the garlic, red pepper flakes and honey and leave to cook for another 5 minutes or so, until the potatoes are golden all over and you can smell the nuttiness.

4. Carefully tip the balls into a serving dish with the butter from the pan, and sprinkle with flaky sea salt, to serve.

FONDANT AUX POMMES

¾ cup/1 cup butter, depending on clarifying method (to give ⅔ cup for the recipe), or ⅔ cup ghee

6 long russet potatoes, peeled and trimmed top and bottom to give flat ends

2 Tbsp olive oil

3 garlic cloves, crushed

5 thyme sprigs, cut into 2-inch spears

generous ¾ cup chicken broth

flaky sea salt, to serve

It's *French*, it's fancy, it's beautiful. If it were a person, it would smoke a cigarette and look down on you. But oh, it's so cool! If you're feeling really posh, you might want to serve it by its proper French name, fondant aux pommes, but on a regular day, the English/French mash-up of pommes fondant does the job, too. I remember little school-level French except for "*C'est bien!*" which is very much the case here. You'll need to make clarified butter: I've given two options for how – choose your favorite.

————

1. To make your clarified butter, either melt the ¾ cup of butter in a small saucepan over a low heat – you want it to just melt, no more. Then, carefully pour the uppermost liquid into a container. As soon as you see the white liquid underneath, stop pouring. You have clarified butter in the container and buttermilk at the bottom of the pan. Or, place 1 cup of butter in a microwave-safe dish. Microwave until melted, but do not stir! Place the container in the fridge to set the butter. Then, poke a hole in the corner and let the milky bit out (that's the buttermilk). Tip out the block of set butter and use a knife to scrape off any leftover buttermilk – there you have your clarified butter. Now you'll just need to melt it down to use.

2. Stand each potato up on one of its flat ends and, using a 1½-inch round cookie cutter, press down from the top to create a cylinder. If you don't have a cookie cutter, neatly cut around the edges with a knife. Keep some of the chunky trimmings for later. Trim the potatoes to make sure they are all the same height (about 2–2½ inches tall) and the top and bottom of each is level.

3. Find a saucepan that's just big enough to fit the potatoes when they are standing on one end (it should be a tight squeeze) and tall enough to be able to cover the potatoes with liquid. Remove the potatoes again, and set aside.

4. Heat the oil in the empty saucepan over a medium heat. Once hot, add the potatoes, least attractive end down, and leave them to color in the pan for 7–10 minutes, until golden. Using some kitchen tongs, flip them over on to the opposite flat end and add your melted, clarified butter (this should come about halfway up the sides of the potatoes), crushed garlic and spears of thyme. If there are any gaps between the potatoes, push some of your potato trimmings into them. There should be no wiggle room. After about 5 minutes, add the broth to cover.

5. Leave the pan over a medium–high heat for about 10 minutes, until the liquid has reduced by around ½ inch. Then, cover the potatoes snugly with a circle of parchment paper. Cook for 40 minutes, or until the potatoes have absorbed all of the liquid and butter and are tender. They should stick slightly to the base of the pan – don't worry. Leave them to cool a bit and they will wiggle free. Turn them up the other way and sprinkle with flaky sea salt to serve.

BACON-WRAPPED FONDANTS

6 long russet
potatoes, peeled
and trimmed top
and bottom to give
flat ends

6 slices of bacon

10 rosemary sprigs

2 Tbsp olive oil

⅔ cup clarified butter
(see page 146)

1 cup chicken broth

6 garlic cloves,
peeled and bashed
but left whole

flaky sea salt,
to serve

Wrap me up in bacon and lay me to rest, because I am DONE. I made this heavenly fondant one Christmas for my family and it's now a festive staple. Over 18 million people on social media apparently agree – having watched me make these fondants online. So, rustle up this viral spud and find out what all the fuss is about. I serve it every Christmas for a reason.

————

1. Stand each potato up on one of its flat ends and, using a 1½-inch round cookie cutter, press down from the top of the potato to create a potato cylinder. If you don't have a cookie cutter, do the best you can do using a knife to cut neatly around the edges. Keep some of the chunky trimmings for later. Trim to make sure the potatoes are all the same height (ideally about 2–2½ inches tall) and the top and bottom of each is as level as possible.

2. Wrap a slice of bacon around each cylinder and secure it by piercing it with a rosemary sprig.

3. Find a saucepan that's just big enough to fit the potatoes when they are standing on one end (it should be a tight squeeze) and tall enough to be able to cover the potatoes with liquid. Remove the potatoes again and set aside.

4. Heat the oil in the empty saucepan over a medium heat. Once hot, add the potatoes, least attractive end down, and leave them to color in the pan for 7–10 minutes, until golden.

5. Using some kitchen tongs, flip them over on to the opposite flat end and add your clarified butter (this should come about halfway up the sides of the potatoes). At this point if there are any gaps between the potatoes, push some of your potato trimmings into them. There should be no wiggle room. After about 5 minutes, add the broth to completely cover the potatoes, then add the garlic and remaining rosemary sprigs.

6. Cover the potatoes with a circle of parchment paper (it should fit snugly into the pan without leaving any gaps at the sides), reduce the heat to medium–low and cook for about 50–60 minutes, until the potatoes have absorbed all the broth and some of the butter, leaving you with super-soft, fluffy potatoes in a pool of caramelized butter.

7. Turn off the heat and leave the spuds in the pan. After about 10–15 minutes, they will wiggle off the bottom. Add a sprinkle of salt and you're good to serve.

FRENCH ONION FONDANTS

6 long russet
potatoes, peeled
and trimmed top
and bottom to give
flat ends

3 Tbsp clarified butter
(see page 146)

1 Tbsp olive oil

1 red onion, sliced

3 garlic cloves,
sliced

3 Tbsp balsamic
vinegar

7 Tbsp white wine

about 1 cup beef
broth

about ¼ cup grated
gruyère

You need to try these immediately. And feel naughty. But good… oh-so good, because not only are they presented with a bubbling gruyère topping, they're also simmered in a rich wine bath. These fondants are the most insanely indulgent potato going.

———

1. Stand each potato up on one of the flat ends and, using a 1½-inch round cookie cutter, press down from the top of the potato to create a potato cylinder. If you don't have a cookie cutter, do the best you can do using a knife to cut around the edges. Keep some of the chunky trimmings for later. Trim to make sure the potatoes are all the same height (ideally about 2–2½ inches tall) and the top and bottom of each is as level as possible.

2. Find a frying pan that's just big enough to fit the potatoes when they are standing on one end (it should be a tight squeeze). Place it over a medium–high heat, add the clarified butter and olive oil together and leave until the butter has melted, the oil is hot and they have combined. Add the potatoes in a single layer and fry them for 10–15 minutes, until golden brown on the underside, then remove them from the pan and set aside on a plate.

3. Add the onion to the same pan and fry for about 7–10 minutes, until it starts to brown and caramelize. Then, add the garlic and cook for a few minutes more, to soften. Deglaze the pan with the balsamic vinegar and white wine, and leave the liquid to reduce until it has almost gone (about 5–10 minutes).

4. Return the potatoes to the pan, browned side up. Pour the beef broth around the sides of the potatoes until only the tops of the potatoes are peeking out – you may not need all the broth or you may need a splash more, depending on your pan. Place a circle of parchment paper over the top of the potatoes to cover, then leave them to bubble away for 30–40 minutes. Remove the parchment and leave the liquid to reduce for another 15–20 minutes, until the broth is sticky around the onions. Turn off the heat and leave to cool for a few minutes to let the potatoes release from the bottom of the pan – don't try to force them, otherwise you'll leave the best bit in the frying pan!

5. Meanwhile, heat the broiler to its hottest setting.

6. Sprinkle the gruyère over the top of the potatoes and put the frying pan under the broiler. Broil for 3–4 minutes, until the cheese is bubbling and golden. Get stuck in.

CLASSIC HASSELBACKS

Serves 2

2 baking potatoes

½ tsp garlic powder

½ tsp white pepper

½ tsp smoked
  paprika

½ tsp salt

crack of black
  pepper

neutral oil

1 Tbsp room-
  temperature butter

The hasselback – also commonly known as the Hasselhoff, or maybe that's just me? That might explain why I get the inexplicable urge to eat these while wearing red swimwear. Despite the 80s reputation, these spuds need a renaissance. If this is the first time you've made a hasselback, ask Alexa to play "David Hasselhoff – Jump in My Car" and crack on for the ride of your life.

———

1. Heat the oven to 400°F.

2. One potato at a time, lay the handles of two wooden spoons either side of the potato, then make vertical cuts all along the length, so that you cut almost through, but the spoon handles stop you going through completely (a fully sliced, collapsed potato is definitely not what we're looking for). Chopsticks will do a good job of this, too, if you have them.

3. In a little mixing bowl, mix those beautiful seasonings, spices, and salt and pepper together.

4. Get the spuds on to a baking sheet and drizzle oil all over. Heavily sprinkle with the spice mixture and place the sheet on the middle shelf of the oven. Bake for 30 minutes, then baste those beauties with the butter and return to the oven for a further 20–25 minutes, until golden, tender and a little crispy.

CARAMELIZED ONION + CREAM CHEESE HASSELBACKS

2 baking potatoes

neutral oil

4 onions, thinly
sliced

2 Tbsp light brown
soft sugar

¼ cup white wine
vinegar

2 Tbsp full-fat cream
cheese (plain or
herbed)

1 Tbsp butter

2 garlic cloves,
minced

salt and black
pepper

I'm a sucker for a caramelized onion, so I had to incorporate that into a crispy, fluffy and cheesy hasselback, oozing with flavor and texture. It really is a delight for the senses. I've come to realize that this book is just an exposé of all my not-so-guilty pleasures.

———

1. Heat the oven to 400°F.

2. One potato at a time, lay the handles of two wooden spoons either side of the potato, then make vertical cuts all along the length so that you cut almost through, but the spoon handles stop you going through completely. Chopsticks will do a good job of this, too, if you have them.

3. Get the potatoes into a baking sheet and drizzle oil all over, rubbing it into those cuts. Heavily sprinkle the potatoes with salt and pepper, then place the baking sheet on the middle shelf and bake the potatoes for 30 minutes, while you make the caramelized onions.

4. Drizzle a little oil into a medium saucepan over a medium heat. When hot, add the onions and fry for 8 minutes, until they have taken on a little color. Mix together the sugar, vinegar and 7 Tbsp of water and add this to the pan. Reduce the heat to medium–low and leave the onions to cook for 20–30 minutes, until golden, tacky and caramelized. Remove from the heat and leave to cool.

5. Put half the cooled onions in a mixing bowl with the cream cheese and stir to combine. In another bowl, add the butter and garlic and mix well.

6. Once the potatoes have been cooking for 30 minutes, spread a little of the oniony cheese filling between each cut, then dot over some garlicky butter. Return the potatoes to the oven for 15–20 minutes, until tender and crisp.

7. Serve with the remaining caramelized onions as a base – 'cause who doesn't like a caramelized onion?

HONEY, MUSTARD + GARLIC HASSELBACKS

Serves 4–6

6 Yukon Gold
  potatoes

neutral oil

1–2 Tbsp room-
  temperature butter

3–4 Tbsp honey

1 tsp Dijon mustard

3 garlic cloves, finely
  grated

salt and black
  pepper

flaky sea salt,
  to serve

This is a shove-it-in-my-face immediately kinda dish. I've eaten my way through about three of these without even realizing before now. Fun fact – this recipe is actually one of my most viral recipes online: over 20 million people have watched it. That's a lot of people.

——

1. Heat the oven to 400°F.

2. One potato at a time, lay the handles of two wooden spoons either side of the potato, then make vertical cuts all along the length so that you cut almost through, but the spoon handles stop you going through completely. Chopsticks will do a good job of this, too, if you have them.

3. Get the potatoes into a baking sheet and drizzle oil all over, rubbing it into those cuts. Heavily sprinkle the potatoes with salt and pepper, then place the baking sheet on the middle shelf and bake the potatoes for 30–40 minutes. Remove the sheet from the oven, brush the potatoes with the butter (gently open the cuts with a knife, just to help get all that buttery goodness inside), and return them to the oven for a further 15 minutes, until golden and cooked all the way through.

4. Towards the end of the cooking time, grab a small saucepan and add the honey, mustard and garlic. Cook over a low–medium heat for 5 minutes, until bubbling.

5. Once the potatoes are ready, evenly pour the honey, mustard and garlic glaze over the top, making sure they all get a good helping. Get them back in the oven for a final 10 minutes, until bubbling, sticky and completely caramelized.

6. Serve up the sticky potatoes with a nice pinch of flaky sea salt, just like the chefs do on the TV.

POPPY'S SNACKLEBACKS

1 lb 2 oz baby white
   potatoes

1 whole head of
   garlic

1 Tbsp neutral oil

1 tsp smoked paprika

5 Tbsp butter, at
   room temperature

salt and black
   pepper

handful of chopped
   chives, to serve
   (optional)

I'm dying on the hill that I invented the word "snackleback" – snack-sized hasselbacks. I'm sure someone will DM me telling me I'm a potato fraud and they first said snackleback in 1066, but I first coined the word in some videos I made for LADBible back in July 2020, so as far as I'm concerned it's mine. Good times – in the comments everyone told me that at first they thought they were slugs. Lovely.

———

1. Heat the oven to 400°F.

2. One potato at a time, lay the handles of two wooden spoons either side of the potato, then make vertical cuts all along the length so that you cut almost through, but the spoon handles stop you going through completely. Chopsticks will do a good job of this, too, if you have them.

3. Cut the top off the head of garlic.

4. Place the potatoes sliced side down in a roasting pan with the garlic, then drizzle with the oil and season with salt and pepper. Bake for 25 minutes, or until your garlic is golden. Remove the pan from the oven, flip your potatoes over and remove the garlic. Put the potatoes back in the oven for a further 15 minutes, or until completely golden and crispy.

5. Squeeze out all your garlic cloves from the skin into a blender, or into a mortar, and add the paprika, butter and a pinch each of salt and pepper to season. Blend or bash everything together to form a fragrant, buttery paste.

6. Brush the potatoes with your buttery paste (save some for dipping, though) and place them back in the oven for a few more minutes, until the butter has sunk into the slits and made the potatoes glistening, golden nuggets. Remove from the oven and sprinkle with your chopped chives to serve, if you like.

Chapter
Six

Baked
Potatoes
+ Skins

STAR-CROSSED GARLIC BAKED POTATOES

2 baking potatoes

neutral oil

1 whole head of
  garlic

pinch of granulated
  sugar

5 Tbsp full-fat cream
  cheese

7 Tbsp butter

small handful of
  Italian parsley,
  leaves chopped

salt and black
  pepper

I took inspo from Korean garlic bread for this, so you have cream cheese and garlic stuffed into your baked potato. It's a beauty. I named it star-crossed because you cross the potato like a star; and because it sounds cool. I know that star-crossed actually means two people in love who are not meant to be together. Thing is, you will fall in love with this potato AND you'll actually be allowed to be together. Whenever you want. Again and again. Romeo and Juliet eat your heart out – I'm re-writing Shakespeare.

1. Heat your oven to 425°F.

2. Rub your potatoes with oil and a good amount of salt, pierce with a fork and then wrap the head of garlic and the potatoes individually in foil. Bake for 45 minutes, until the spuds and garlic are cooked, then remove the foil and the garlic. Return the potatoes to the oven for another 5–15 minutes, until the skins are crispy and the flesh is tender.

3. Meanwhile, make the filling. In a mixing bowl, mix together the sugar and cream cheese and season with salt and pepper.

4. In a separate bowl, melt your butter in a microwave until just softened and stir through your chopped parsley. Squeeze out the garlic from the skins; it should be soft enough to smush with a fork, then add that to the butter, too.

5. Remove the potatoes from the oven and cut six deep slits in the top in the shape of a star (take care not to cut all the whole way through). Fill your slits with the cheese mixture, then douse the top in garlic-parsley butter and sprinkle over some more salt.

6. Turn up your oven to 450°F and throw those spuds back in for 15–20 minutes, until they are extra-crispy.

NOTE

These potatoes are perfect for the air fryer! Cook for 45 minutes on 400°F, then fill them and put them back in to give them a final 10 minutes at the end.

CHORIZO-LOADED BAKED POTATOES

2 baking potatoes

neutral oil

5 oz-ish spicy uncooked chorizo sausage, diced or crumbled

2 Tbsp full-fat cream cheese, or more if you like

few pats of butter

small handful of Italian parsley, leaves chopped

squeeze of lemon juice

salt and black pepper

This spud is me all over: baked, stuffed and salty AF. Aside from that, this filling is delicious and goes that kinda orange color that you know is full of flavor. The chorizo-infused cream cheese is a combo you never knew you needed, but trust me, you do. These are a perfect stand-alone midweek meal. I usually serve them up with some broccolini, or with asparagus when it's in season.

———

1. Heat your oven to 425°F.

2. Rub your potatoes with oil and a good amount of salt, and pierce them all over with a fork. Place them on a rack in the middle of your oven and bake for about 50–60 minutes, until tender on the inside and crispy on the outside.

3. Once your potatoes are 20 minutes from being ready, you can start on the filling.

4. Add the chopped chorizo to a cold frying pan and get it over a medium heat. After about 5 minutes, all of that beautiful red fat should have rendered out. Once this has happened, remove the pan from the heat.

5. Tip the cream cheese into a mixing bowl, then strain the chorizo fat through a strainer into the bowl. Mix well to combine.

6. When the potatoes are done, slice them open and fork the middle to fluff up the flesh. Add the butter and a quarter of the fried chorizo pieces into each potato. Then, add half the cream-cheese mixture on top. Finish with the remaining fried chorizo, a sprinkle of parsley and a squeeze of lemon. F**king fabulous. Enjoy!

SALT-BAKED POTATOES

1½ lbs coarse sea salt or coarse kosher salt (about 2⅓ cups)

3 egg whites

2 baking potatoes

few pats of butter

During my time working in restaurants, we'd have salt-baked fish on the menu and even salt-baked baby potatoes, but never a BIG SALT-BAKED POTATO. And, honestly, I'm wowing. It makes the skin of the potato a lovely hard, salty, savory deliciousness. It's not the most crispy, but it doesn't need to be. I slather mine with butter and dig in. Heavenly!

――――

1. Start by making a salt crust. Simply mix the salt with the egg whites. At this point you can also add herbs like rosemary and thyme. Or lemon zest or whole spices to help infuse flavor, but I'm keeping it super-simple by just using salt this time.

2. Heat the oven to 400°F.

3. Line a rimmed baking sheet big enough for both potatoes with parchment paper. Add a layer of the salt mixture, place the potatoes on top, then cover with the rest of the salt. (You can also use little potatoes in this recipe and make more of them, if you prefer.)

4. Once the potatoes are completely covered in salt, place the baking sheet on the middle shelf and bake the potatoes for 1½ hours. You may need a bit more or less, depending on the size of your potatoes (go with 1½ hours and keep an eye on the action) – look for when the salt crust has turned a caramel brown, then poke a long, sharp knife into the salt crust and through to the potato flesh. If they are ready, the potatoes should feel soft all the way through.

5. Remove the potatoes from the oven and, using a rolling pin or a heavy blunt instrument, crack open the salty shell. The potatoes will be very hot, so just be careful.

6. Once you have released the potatoes from their salty prison, cut them open and fork through the middle to fluff them up. Add a pat of butter and whichever potato topping you fancy (I've given you my favorite, below).

MY FAVORITE TOPPING

A classic: coleslaw and cheese. Thinly shred ½ green cabbage, 1 peeled carrot and ½ onion, then finely chop a handful of Italian parsley. Mix together 2 Tbsp of mayo and 1 tsp of Dijon mustard, and season with salt and pepper. Mix the dressing through the vegetables and shovel the lot on top of the potatoes with a load of shredded cheese.

SHRIMP PO' BOY BAKED POTATO WITH COLESLAW

2 baking potatoes

neutral oil

7 Tbsp buttermilk

1 tsp smoked paprika

1 tsp Italian seasoning

1 tsp garlic powder

1 tsp onion powder

½ tsp ground black pepper

8–10 large, raw, shell-off and deveined shrimp

⅓ cup plus 1 Tbsp all-purpose flour

few pats of butter

FOR THE COLESLAW

⅛ small red cabbage, thinly shredded

⅛ small green cabbage, thinly shredded

½ carrot, peeled and julienned

2 tsp white wine vinegar

2 tsp olive oil

small handful of Italian parsley, leaves chopped

small handful of chives, chopped

salt and black pepper

FOR THE SAUCE

2 Tbsp mayo

1 Tbsp ketchup

squeeze of lemon juice

dash of Tabasco

dash of Worcestershire sauce

Enter the collab of the century: shrimp and baked potatoes. You might be partial to a basic bit of shrimp cocktail on your spud, but I've amped it up by taking some of the flavors of a New Orlean's po' boy and creating the shrimp potato of dreams. If you need me, I'll be sat alone in the corner demolishing one of these beauties.

____

1. Heat the oven to 425°F.

2. Rub your potatoes with oil and a good amount of salt, and pierce them all over with a fork. Place them on a rack in the middle of the oven and bake for about 50–60 minutes, until tender on the inside and crisp on the outside.

3. While the potatoes are baking, make the coleslaw. Mix together all the veggies in a bowl. In another bowl, combine the white wine vinegar, olive oil and herbs. Pour the dressing over the cabbage mixture and turn to coat. Season to taste with salt and pepper and set aside for later.

4. Make the sauce by mixing together all the ingredients in a bowl, seasoning with salt and pepper, then tasting and adjusting the ingredients to your preference. Set aside.

5. Once the potatoes are almost ready, season the buttermilk with salt and pepper and ½ tsp each of the smoked paprika, Italian seasoning, garlic powder and onion powder, and ¼ tsp of the ground black pepper, then tip in the shrimp. In a bowl, combine the flour, a big pinch of salt to season, and the remaining smoked paprika, Italian seasoning, garlic and onion powder, and pepper.

6. Pour your oil into a deep fryer or a heavy-based saucepan (don't let it come more than halfway up the inside of the pan). Place the pan over a high heat and get the oil to 350°F on a candy thermometer (or use the thermometer in your fryer).

7. Sprinkle 1 Tbsp of the seasoned buttermilk into the flour and stir to form some clumps that will go super-crispy. Shake off the excess buttermilk and, in batches, coat the shrimp in the flour and fry for about 1–2 minutes, until golden brown, crispy and cooked through. Set each batch aside to drain on paper towel while you fry the remainder, then season lightly with salt.

8. Slice the potatoes lengthways down the middle, open them up slightly and fork in the butter to melt. Top with a large dollop of the coleslaw, and crown with a few of those crispy shrimp and a drizzle of sauce.

BEEF BRISKET CHILI-LOADED BAKED POTATOES

Serves 4

4 baking potatoes

neutral oil

few pats of butter

FOR THE CHILI

olive oil

2 slices thick-cut
  bacon, diced

1 lb beef brisket, cut
  into 1½-inch cubes

onion powder,
  to sprinkle

garlic powder,
  to sprinkle

smoked paprika,
  to sprinkle

1 onion, finely
  chopped

½ green bell pepper,
  seeded and diced

2 garlic cloves, sliced

¾ cup plus 1 Tbsp
  strong coffee

1 tsp ground cumin

½ tsp cayenne
  pepper

1 x 14-oz can of diced
  tomatoes

1¼ cups beef broth

salt and black pepper

TO GARNISH

sour cream

sliced pickled
  jalapeños

shredded extra-
  sharp cheddar

sliced scallions

It's got to be up there as one of the top baked-potato fillings hasn't it? Chili con carne. Nothing beats warm chili, melting cheese, all nestled into a beautifully crisp baked potato. I've levelled it up with a beef brisket chili on top, because if you can't go extra-fancy with a baked potato, when can you?

———

1. Make the chili. To a large saucepan over a high heat, add a drizzle of olive oil and fry off the bacon until golden. Remove from the pan and set aside. In batches, fry the beef brisket until golden brown all over (about 2–3 minutes, turning), seasoning each batch with a sprinkling of about ¼ tsp of onion powder, garlic powder and smoked paprika, and a pinch each of salt and pepper. Set aside each batch on a plate while you fry the remainder, then remove the last batch and set it all aside.

2. Add a bit more oil to the same pan, if needed, and sweat the onion and bell pepper together for 4–5 minutes to soften. Add the garlic and cook for another few minutes. Pour in the coffee to deglaze the pan and chuck in the ground cumin and cayenne pepper. Add the canned tomatoes and half fill the empty can with water and add that, too.

3. Add the beef and bacon back to the pan, then finally add the beef broth. Give everything a good stir and season well with salt and pepper. Leave to simmer on the stove for 2½–3 hours, until the brisket is falling apart.

4. When you've got about 1 hour left of cooking time on your chili, heat the oven to 425°F.

5. Rub your potatoes with oil and a good amount of salt, and pierce them all over with a fork. Place them on a rack in the middle of the oven and bake for about 50–60 minutes, until tender on the inside and crisp on the outside.

6. Cut a cross in the middle of each potato. Press the sides together to open up each potato and fork in the butter to melt. Spoon over a big scoop of the chili, then serve topped with sour cream, jalapeños, cheddar and scallions, to your liking.

170

BACON SOUR-CREAM BAKED POTATOES

2 baking potatoes

olive oil

4 slices of bacon

2 pats of butter

handful of shredded
  pizza blend cheese
  or a mixture of
  shredded cheddar
  and shredded
  mozzarella

2 heaping Tbsp sour
  cream

2 scallions, thinly sliced

salt and black pepper

You've gotta love a classic. There's no fancy schmancy, hard-to-find ingredients in this recipe – just stacks of meaty, cheesy, creamy goodness. This one is a proper crowd-pleaser. Simple and delicious.

———

1. Heat the oven to 425°F.

2. Rub your potatoes with oil and a good amount of salt, and pierce them all over with a fork. Place them on a rack in the middle of the oven and bake for about 50–60 minutes, until tender on the inside and crisp on the outside.

3. Meanwhile, heat a frying pan over a medium–high heat. Add the bacon and fry for 3–4 minutes, until completely crispy. Remove from the pan and chop half the bacon into small pieces so that it is almost crumbled. Leave the remainder whole to use as a garnish later.

4. Cut a cross into the top of each baked potato and use a fork to mash up the inside of each with a pat of butter. Sprinkle on one quarter of the bacon bits and half the cheese per potato, then return the potatoes to the oven. Switch the setting to broil and leave the cheese to melt until golden and bubbling.

5. Remove the potatoes from the oven and top them with a big spoonful of sour cream and some more bacon bits and your reserved whole rashers, then finish with a sprinkle of sliced scallions.

Potato Lovers...

You're Safe Here.

CLASSIC POTATO SKINS

4 baking potatoes

neutral oil

4 slices of smoked
   bacon, cut into
   little pieces; or
   8–10 baby bella
   mushrooms, sliced,
   for a veggie option

1 cup shredded
   mozzarella

1 cup shredded mild
   cheddar

2 scallions, sliced

salt and black
   pepper

TO SERVE

sour cream

yellow mustard

ketchup

You can't beat a classic potato skin. I've spoken about it time and again, but when I was growing up every year I'd spend my birthday at TGI Friday's and the whole family would just eat appetizers. That, to me, is the best kinda meal – appetizers, picky bits, dips and chips, everyone sharing. Heaven. Don't judge me for this, but ten-year-old Poppy invented the best thing to top your potato skins and I still do it to this day: a squeeze of ketchup, a squeeze of mustard and a good, thick sour-cream dollop. Mix it together and it goes like an orangey weird color but, oh my! It's incredible.

_____

1. Heat the oven to 425°F.

2. Rub your potatoes with oil and a good amount of salt, and pierce them all over with a fork. Place them on a rack in the middle of the oven and bake for about 50–60 minutes, until tender on the inside and crisp on the outside.

3. While the potatoes are baking, heat a frying pan over a medium–high heat and add the bacon. Fry for 5 minutes, until crispy all over (or, fry the mushrooms in a little oil).

4. Once the potatoes are ready, remove them from the oven and whack the heat up to 450°F. You can up the temperature even more, if you like your skins crissssspy.

5. Cut all your potatoes in half and scoop out the flesh, so you're left with an even-ish layer of potato and skin (you can make this as thick or as thin as you like). You won't need the flesh for this recipe, but keep it and use it for fish cakes, hash browns and so on.

6. Place the empty skins on a wire rack, place them in the oven and bake for 10 minutes, to crisp up. Once crispy, remove from the oven and fill the skins equally with the mozzarella, bacon and cheddar. Then, return them to the oven for around 5–10 minutes to melt the cheese.

7. Once they are ready, sprinkle them with scallions, and finally slap on some sour cream, mustard and ketchup, to serve. It is élite.

CAULIFLOWER GRATIN SKINS

4 baking potatoes

olive oil

½ large cauliflower
or 1 small, broken
into small florets

2 Tbsp butter

2 Tbsp all-purpose
flour

1 cup–1¼ cups whole
milk

1 tsp Dijon mustard

2 thyme sprigs,
leaves picked

grating of fresh
nutmeg

½ cup shredded
extra-sharp
cheddar

½ cup shredded
gruyère or comté

salt and black
pepper

At first you might think… that's a bit different. Maybe you're not too sure about the sound of it. Maybe the thought of a cauliflower in a potato intrigues you. Maybe it scares you. Well, trust me on this. This potato skin is absolutely INCREDIBLE. And this dish would be delicious on the plate with any roast meat. Let's promote potato skins from sharing appetizers to having pride of place at that Sunday dinner with your family. Enjoy.

———

1. Heat the oven to 425°F.

2. Rub your potatoes with oil and a good amount of salt, and pierce them all over with a fork. Place them on a rack in the middle of the oven and bake for about 50–60 minutes, until tender on the inside and crisp on the outside.

3. Meanwhile, tip the florets into a rimmed baking sheet and drizzle them with olive oil. Season with salt and pepper, then roast for 15–20 minutes, until golden brown.

4. While the potatoes and cauliflower are cooking, melt the butter in a small saucepan over a medium heat and add the flour. Whisk them together to a paste and cook for a few minutes to cook out the flour. Then, gradually pour in the milk, bringing to a boil between each addition, until your sauce is smooth with a thick pouring consistency (you may not need all the milk).

5. Add the Dijon mustard, thyme leaves and a good grating of nutmeg, and then stir through the cheeses (but reserve a little of each for the top), to melt.

6. Cut all your potatoes in half and scoop out the flesh, so you are left with an even-ish layer of potato and skin (you can make this as thick or as thin as you like). Mash the scooped flesh in a bowl and, when the cauliflower is ready, add the florets and cheese sauce to the bowl and stir everything together.

7. Increase the oven to 450°F.

8. Spoon the potato and cauliflower mixture into the skins and top with the reserved grated cheese, then place on a baking sheet and roast them in the oven for 15–20 minutes, until golden.

PIZZA-LOADED SKINS

Makes 6

3 baking potatoes

olive oil

1 shallot, diced

2 garlic cloves, finely grated

3 Tbsp balsamic vinegar

1 x 14-oz can of diced tomatoes

1⅔ cups shredded pizza blend cheese or a mixture of shredded cheddar and shredded mozzarella

salt and black pepper

FOR THE TOPPINGS

pepperoni slices

sliced mushrooms

sliced pickled jalapeños

pitted olives

hot honey (see page 182)

...whatever you like on your pizza!

It just makes sense doesn't it? The crispy shell of a potato skin, loaded with scooped-out potato flesh, tomato, cheese and pepperoni. Like a little potato pizza. Kids will love them; adults will fight over them; everyone will be wanting a taste of your cheeky little pizza-skin potatoes.

———

1. Heat the oven to 425°F.

2. Rub your potatoes with oil and a good amount of salt, and pierce them all over with a fork. Place them on a rack in the middle of the oven and bake for about 50–60 minutes, until tender on the inside and crisp on the outside.

3. While the potatoes are baking, get a saucepan over a medium heat and add in plenty of olive oil. Add the shallot and fry for 3–4 minutes, until light golden and soft. Add the garlic and fry for a few minutes to soften, then deglaze the pan with the balsamic vinegar and add the canned tomatoes. Season with salt and pepper and leave to reduce and bubble away until thickened – about 15–20 minutes.

4. Once the potatoes are ready, remove them from the oven (but leave the oven on), cut them in half and scoop out the flesh, so you are left with an even-ish layer of potato and skin (you can make this as thick or as thin as you like). You won't need the flesh for this recipe, but keep it and use it for fish cakes, hash browns and so on.

5. Increase the oven to 450°F.

6. Spoon the tomato sauce into the skins and top with pepperoni, mushrooms or whichever toppings you like to use. Sprinkle with the cheese and place the skins on a baking sheet. Bake for a further 10–15 minutes, until the cheese is melted, bubbling and golden.

HOT HONEY, BURRATA + TOMATO TWICE-BAKED POTATOES

2 baking potatoes

olive oil

7 oz (about 1⅓ cups) cherry or grape tomatoes

3 Tbsp butter

½ cup shredded extra-sharp cheddar

6 oz fresh burrata

salt and black pepper

FOR THE HOT HONEY

1 red chili (such as Fresno), sliced, seeds and all

2 garlic cloves, sliced

scant ⅓ cup honey

We've all had an everyday cheese-and-tomato potato skin, so now it's time to take it to the next level: enter the burrata, roasted tomato and hot honey potato skin. We're dialing everything up to 11 with this one, and it's sooooo worth it. The hot honey (as in with a bit of spice, not like Spain in August) adds an extra kick to these decadent little beauties.

———

1. Heat the oven to 425°F.

2. Rub your potatoes with oil and a good amount of salt, and pierce them all over with a fork. Place them on a rack in the middle of the oven and bake for about 50–60 minutes, until tender on the inside and crisp on the outside.

3. When the potatoes are almost cooked, get the tomatoes into a baking sheet, season well with salt and pepper and drizzle with olive oil. Bake these in the oven for the last 15–20 minutes of the potato cooking time, until blistered and colored.

4. When the potatoes are ready, remove them from the oven, cut them in half and scoop out the majority of the flesh in each half into a mixing bowl. Set aside.

5. Add the butter, cheddar and half the roasted tomatoes to the bowl with the potato flesh and season with salt and pepper. Mash the mixture together with a fork. Divide the mixture equally between the potato skins so that they are about two-thirds full (any leftovers are cook's perks – dig in) and transfer them to a baking sheet. Add the remaining tomatoes on top.

6. Heat the broiler to high.

7. Divide the burrata into four portions (which is messy, but just roll with it), and place a quarter on top of each potato. Get the potatoes under the broiler to get a bit of color – about 10 minutes.

8. In that time, make your hot honey. Mix all your honey ingredients together in a small saucepan over a medium heat, until the honey starts to bubble, then set aside.

9. Once the burrata has fully melted and has a little color, remove the baking sheet from the broiler. Transfer the skins to serving plates, spoon over some hot honey, and serve.

Makes 6

SPICY CRAB TWICE-BAKED POTATOES WITH MANGO SALSA

3 baking potatoes

neutral oil

4 oz fresh crab meat
(preferably a mixture
of 60% jumbo lump
and 40% claw)

1 generous Tbsp
butter

½ red chili (such as
Fresno), seeded and
finely diced

zest and juice of
1 lemon

small handful of
chives, chopped

2 Tbsp thick crème
fraîche or sour cream

1 tsp garam masala

salt and black pepper

lime wedges, to serve

**FOR THE MANGO
SALSA**

1 medium mango,
peeled, pitted and
cut into ¼-inch cubes

½ small red onion,
finely chopped

1 tsp mango (Major
Grey's) chutney

zest and juice of 1 lime

small handful of
cilantro, leaves
chopped

½ red chili (such as
Fresno), seeded and
finely diced

As a kid, I was addicted to imitation crab sticks. You know – those little red-and-white sticks of crabby goodness. Loved them. Until, that is, someone told me that there's no crab in them at all. That's no fun. Anyway, we're not missing any crab here. Brown claw meat can be harder to find but is worth looking for and here is baked in the spud, with the white lump meat on top. But if you can't find the claw meat then use all lump meat. Delicious.

——

1. Heat the oven to 425°F.

2. Rub your potatoes with oil and a good amount of salt, and pierce them all over with a fork. Place them on a rack in the middle of the oven and bake for about 50–60 minutes, until tender on the inside and crisp on the outside.

3. Halve the potatoes and scoop out the middle into a mixing bowl, leaving about ⅛ inch of potato inside to give some structure. Set aside.

4. Measure out about ½ cup of the reserved potato flesh and add in the brown claw meat, along with the butter, half the diced chili, half the lemon zest and juice, the chives, 1 Tbsp of the crème fraîche and the tsp of garam masala. Season with salt and pepper, then mix well, taste, and season again with salt and pepper accordingly.

5. Divide the potato mixture equally back into the potato skins. Transfer the loaded skins to a baking sheet and bake them in the oven for 15 minutes, until hot through.

6. While the loaded skins are baking, make the salsa. Mix together the mango, onion, mango chutney, lime zest and juice and cilantro and the diced red chili. Season with salt and pepper to taste.

7. Mix the white lump meat in a small bowl with the remaining crème fraîche, red chili, lemon zest and lemon juice and season with salt and pepper. Set aside.

8. Once the crab-filled spuds are baked and slightly crispy on top, remove them from the oven. Top them with the lump meat mixture and a spoonful of mango salsa, and serve with a wedge of lime. They are light, refreshing and super-satisfying.

CHEESE + CHIVE SKIN WEDGES

4 baking potatoes

neutral oil

handful of shredded pizza blend cheese or a mixture of shredded cheddar and shredded mozzarella

2 Tbsp sour cream

small bunch of chives, chopped

pinch of ground ginger

juice of ½ lime

salt and black pepper

Put down the quiche and pick up a cheese-and-chive potato skin, because this is delivering all the picnic vibes. I want my finger foods dripping in cheese, full of carbs and with a hint of greenery. Delicious served both hot and cold and an absolute summer staple.

____

1. Heat the oven to 425°F.

2. Rub your potatoes with oil and a good amount of salt, and pierce them all over with a fork. Place them on a rack in the middle of the oven and bake for about 50–60 minutes, until tender on the inside and crisp on the outside. Keep the oven on.

3. Halve the potatoes and scoop out the middle (keep the flesh for hash browns or fish cakes), leaving about ⅛ inch of potato inside to give some structure. Halve the skins again to give you skin wedges.

4. Pour your oil into a deep fryer or a heavy-based saucepan (don't let it come more than halfway up the inside of the pan). Place the pan over a high heat and get the oil to 350°F on a candy thermometer (or use the thermometer in your fryer).

5. In batches, fry the skins for 2 minutes, until they are golden brown and crunchy. Set aside each batch to drain on paper towel while you fry the remainder.

6. Lay the crispy skins out over a baking sheet and sprinkle over the shredded cheese. Bake in the oven until the cheese is bubbling and golden (about 3–5 minutes).

7. In a small bowl, stir together the sour cream, three-quarters of the chopped chives, the ground ginger and the lime juice. Season to taste with salt and pepper, then spoon this over the skins when they come out of the oven (or use as a dip if eating cold). Sprinkle over the rest of the chives to finish.

Chapter Seven

Potato Salads

CLASSIC POTATO SALAD

Serves 4

1 lb 2 oz baby white potatoes

3 Tbsp mayonnaise

1 tsp grainy mustard (optional)

small handful of Italian parsley, leaves chopped

small handful of chives, chopped

½ shallot, finely diced

salt and black pepper

I dedicated a full section to the potato salad because it's often neglected. I know the dreaded "S" word can put people off. "A salad? I bought this book for some spud-loving, not for salads!" Well, who can reject a salad that is 80-per-cent spud? It's the best kind of diet. I'm on a salad diet at the moment. Just potato salads all day, every day. It's the best.

————

1. Tip your potatoes into a saucepan of heavily salted, cold water. Place the pan over a high heat and bring the water to a boil. Boil the potatoes for 15–20 minutes, until they fall off the tip of a knife. Drain in a colander and leave to cool completely.

2. In a large bowl, mix together the mayonnaise, mustard (if using), parsley, chives and shallot and a big pinch each of salt and pepper. Slice the potatoes in half, mix them through the mayonnaise mixture and dig in!

BACON-LOADED POTATO SALAD

Serves 4

1 lb 2 oz baby white potatoes

7 oz thick-cut bacon, diced

handful of shredded extra-sharp cheddar

2 scallions, thinly sliced

⅓ cup sour cream

salt and black pepper

If there's one bit of advice for making delicious potato dishes even more delicious, it's add bacon. Potato salad is one of those dishes that can really take on a whole new form with some cheeky bacon running through it. I've been extra-naughty with this salad and added cheese, too. That's because you can never forget the second rule for making potato dishes even better – add cheese.

——

1. Tip your potatoes into a saucepan of heavily salted, cold water. Place the pan over a high heat and bring the water to a boil. Boil the potatoes for 15–20 minutes, until they fall off the tip of a knife. Drain in a colander.

2. Grab a frying pan and place it over a medium–high heat. Add the bacon and fry for 5–8 minutes, until golden. Add the potatoes and crush them into the bacon, using a fork or heavy mixing spoon until they are just crushed, and coated in delicious bacon fat. Then, remove from the heat, pour the sour cream over and add the cheese and scallions. Season well with salt and pepper and stir it all together. Then, you can dig right in.

TIP: SALTING WATER

When boiling potatoes (or any veg or pasta, in fact) the water should be as salty as the sea. This triggers osmosis – Google how that works, but it's a good thing, and means you'll need less seasoning overall. Don't worry – not all of the salt is absorbed into the potatoes, so you're not eating it. It just makes the results taste much nicer. In this case, salty water is good for you.

CORONATION-SPICED POTATO SALAD

1 lb 2 oz baby white
  potatoes

3 large Tbsp
  mayonnaise

1 Tbsp mild curry
  powder

pinch of turmeric

squeeze of lemon
  juice

1 scallion, sliced

small handful of
  cilantro, leaves
  chopped (optional)

small handful of
  raisins or golden
  raisins

salt and black
  pepper

This dish is the perfect blend of potato salad and that mildly curried sandwich filling that the Brits adore – coronation chicken. Adding raisins to a dish will always raise an eyebrow, but just imagine them as small pops of sweet freshness that sing summer deliciousness. Yes, it's sweet on savory. Yes, it's fruit. But it works. Is this a bad time to mention I love pineapple on pizza?

———

1. Place your potatoes in a saucepan of heavily salted, cold water. Get the pan over a high heat and bring the water to a boil. Boil the potatoes for 15–20 minutes, until they fall off the tip of a knife. Drain in a colander and leave until cool enough to handle.

2. Meanwhile, gather up the remaining ingredients and mix them together in a large bowl. Taste, and adjust the seasoning with salt and pepper to your liking.

3. Once the potatoes are cool, halve each one and add them to the bowl with your coronation mixture, then give them a good few turns to get them all coated in that creamy goodness!

EGG + CAPER POTATO SALAD

Serves 4

½ Tbsp granulated sugar

5 Tbsp white wine vinegar

1 tsp black peppercorns

1 shallot, sliced into rings

1 lb 2 oz baby white potatoes

2 heaping Tbsp mayonnaise

1 Tbsp capers, roughly chopped

2 eggs, hardboiled and chopped

small handful of Italian parsley, leaves chopped (optional)

salt and black pepper

Oooo, she's a fancy potato salad, this one! Loosely based on a Russian salad, this is for the sophisticated BBQs where you want to show off with an egg or two, too. Capers are an absolute favorite of mine, and add lovely little bursts of salty, savory flavor in every bite.

————

1. Measure 5 Tbsp of water into a saucepan and add the sugar, vinegar, peppercorns and a big pinch of salt. Place the pan over a high heat and bring the liquid to a boil. Meanwhile, tip the shallot rings into a heatproof bowl. Remove the pan from the heat, then pour the hot liquid and all the flavorings over the shallots. Leave to cool (if you have any pickled shallots left over after you've made the salad, they will keep in the fridge for up to three months).

2. Place your potatoes in a saucepan of heavily salted, cold water. Get the pan over a high heat and bring the water to a boil. Boil the potatoes for 15–20 minutes, until they fall off the tip of a knife. Drain in a colander and leave to cool completely.

3. Meanwhile, drain your pickled shallots and tip them into a large mixing bowl with the mayonnaise, capers, eggs and parsley (if using). Taste and adjust the seasoning with salt and pepper to your liking.

4. Once the potatoes are cool, halve each one and add them to the bowl with your egg mixture, then give them a good stir to get them coated in all that flavor.

GREEN GODDESS POTATO SALAD

1 lb 2 oz baby white potatoes

small bunch of Italian parsley (about 1 oz), stalks removed

small bunch of chives (about 1 oz)

4–5 dill sprigs

4–5 mint sprigs, leaves picked, plus optional extra to garnish

1 Tbsp capers, drained

zest and juice of ½ lemon

3 Tbsp full-fat cream cheese

2–3 Tbsp olive oil

2 Tbsp pine nuts, toasted

1 x 2-oz can of anchovies, drained and roughly chopped

½ shallot, finely sliced

2 scallions, thinly sliced

salt and black pepper

Although my aim was to keep this recipe book as beige as physically possible, a little greenery may have slipped in. The closest I'll ever get to a detox. This potato salad is deceptively light and refreshing, and has a tangy twist that makes it the perfect spring dish. Sprinkle through some pine nuts and you're good to go.

———

1. Tip the potatoes into a saucepan of cold, heavily salted water. Place the pan over a high heat and bring the water to a boil. Boil the potatoes for 15–20 minutes, until they fall off the tip of a knife. Drain in a colander and leave to cool completely.

2. In a small blender, add all of the herbs, along with the capers, lemon zest and juice and cream cheese. Season well with salt and pepper, then blitz until smooth, dribbling in the olive oil and a splash of water to loosen and help everything blend. Taste for seasoning and set aside.

3. Slice the potatoes into large chunks and put them into a large bowl with the pine nuts, anchovies, shallot and scallions. Spoon over the dressing and toss everything together to coat. You can sprinkle a little extra chopped mint on top, too, if you like.

DILL + PICKLE POTATO SALAD

1 lb 2 oz baby white
  potatoes

juice of 1 lime

2 tsp Dijon mustard

splash of cornichon/
  dill pickle juice

1 Tbsp sweet relish

1 tsp white wine
  vinegar

about 7 Tbsp olive oil

2 cornichons or
  2 dill pickle spears,
  sliced

small handful of
  dill, torn

¼ English cucumber,
  seeded and
  chopped

½ red onion, thinly
  sliced

salt and black
  pepper

Okay, it needs to be known... I am an absolute pickle fiend.
I love all things pickle. Maybe if I weren't a potato queen,
I would be a pickle princess. Everything pickle is a big yes
in my book: carrots, cucumbers, cabbage, walnuts and even
eggs. Dill pickles are the star of this potato salad, which is the
result of two of my favorite things marrying together in perfect
pickly potato heaven.

——

1. Place your potatoes in a saucepan of heavily salted, cold water. Get the
   pan over a high heat and bring the water to a boil. Boil the potatoes for
   15–20 minutes, until they fall off the tip of a knife. Drain in a colander and
   leave until cool enough to handle.

2. Mix together the lime juice, mustard, cornichon/pickle juice, relish and
   vinegar and slowly drizzle in the olive oil until the mixture reaches a
   vinaigrette consistency.

3. Meanwhile, gather up the remaining ingredients and mix them together in a
   large bowl. Taste and adjust the seasoning with salt and pepper to your liking.

4. Once the potatoes are cool, halve or quarter each one and add the halves
   to the bowl with your vinaigrette and the rest of your ingredients, then give
   them a good mix to combine.

VIRAL CRISPY POTATO SALAD

1 lb 2 oz baby white
  potatoes

1½ tsp smoked
  paprika

1 tsp onion powder

1 tsp garlic powder

1 tsp dried parsley

1 tsp dried rosemary

1 tsp salt

¼ cup olive oil

**FOR THE
DRESSING**

2 Tbsp mayonnaise

1 Tbsp sour cream

1 heaping tsp Dijon
  mustard

1 Tbsp sliced pickled
  shallots, drained
  (see page 197)

1 scallion, sliced

small handful of
  chives, chopped

small handful of
  Italian parsley,
  leaves roughly
  chopped

salt and black
  pepper

That's right, a potato salad can be crispy, and boy has this got CROUNCH. This is a viral recipe that is rightfully viral. It's time to take your next BBQ to new heights, because not only will this become the star side, it will distract your guests when you burn the second lot of sausages.

———

1. Tip the potatoes into a saucepan of heavily salted, cold water. Place the pan over a high heat and bring the water to a boil. Boil the potatoes for 15–20 minutes, until they fall off the tip of a knife. Drain in a colander and leave to cool slightly.

2. Meanwhile, heat the oven to 400°F. Mix together all of the dried spices, seasonings and dried herbs with the salt and plenty of black pepper. Stir in the oil and set aside.

3. Tip the potatoes into a large rimmed baking sheet (you may need two) and, using the base of a jar or can, squash the potatoes gently so that they flatten out. Use a pastry brush or the back of a spoon to spread the spiced oil mixture all over the potatoes.

4. Put the potatoes in the oven for around 45–50 minutes, turning once halfway through, until they are golden brown and crispy.

5. In a large mixing bowl, mix together all of the dressing ingredients and season well with salt and pepper.

6. Just before serving (again, the timing is important – any sooner and the crispy bits will go soft), toss the crispy potatoes through the dressing and serve straight away.

Chapter Eight

Easy Potato Bakes

LEEKY POTATO BAKE

1¾ lbs baking
potatoes, peeled
and sliced into
½-inch rounds

1 Tbsp neutral oil

2 leeks, sliced
1 inch thick

3 Tbsp butter

½ large shallot, finely
chopped (optional)

3 garlic cloves,
chopped

⅓ cup plus 1 Tbsp
all-purpose flour

1¼ cups whole milk

7 Tbsp heavy cream

heaping ¾ cup
shredded gruyère

1 cup shredded
extra-sharp
cheddar

pinch of ground
nutmeg

2 handfuls of
shredded pizza
blend cheese
or a mixture of
shredded cheddar
and shredded
mozzarella

salt and black
pepper

Whenever I think of the combo of cheesy leeks and potatoes, I think of my mother-in-law, who makes a leeky bake every Sunday as a side for dinner. It's now become a staple in my Sunday dinner, too, as you really cannot beat the cheesy leeky goodness on the side of your plate. And, of course, you have to have it AS WELL AS your roasted potatoes, not instead of. Potatoes on potatoes.

_____

1. Get the potato slices into a large saucepan of heavily salted, cold water. Place the pan over a high heat and bring the water to a boil. Reduce the heat and leave on a gentle boil for 8 minutes, until the potatoes fall off the tip of a knife. Drain in a colander and leave to the side.

2. To the same pan, add the oil and get it over a high heat. Add the leeks and fry for 5 minutes, until soft and golden. Scoop them out and set them aside.

3. Heat the oven to 400°F.

4. Reduce the heat under the leek pan a little and melt the butter. Add the shallot (if using) and garlic and, once the butter is foamy, stir in the flour. Cook out the flour, stirring, until it forms almost a dough.

5. Mix the milk and cream together in a pitcher, then add it a little at a time to the pan, stirring constantly, until you have added all the milk mixture. This should take a good 7–10 minutes. Add the gruyère, cheddar and nutmeg and season with salt and pepper.

6. Layer half the potatoes in the bottom of an ovenproof dish (see tip, below, for how to find the right size), then top them with half the leeks. Cover with half the sauce. Repeat, using the remaining ingredients in the same order. Scatter over the shredded cheese, then very loosely place some foil on top – don't let it touch the cheesiness.

7. Bake the potatoes and leeks in the oven for 30 minutes. Remove the foil and bake for a further 20–30 minutes, until golden and bubbling.

**TIP: HOW TO FIND THE
RIGHT SIZE OVENPROOF DISH**

I judge the size of dish I need by putting the right number of whole, uncooked potatoes into a chosen dish and, once they fit snugly, I know that's the dish for me. It's like Cinderella, but for potatoes.

AUSSIE-INSPIRED BAKE

Serves 4

1¾ lbs Yukon Gold
  potatoes, peeled
  and sliced into
  ½-inch rounds

5 slices thick-cut
  bacon, diced

2 garlic cloves,
  minced

⅔ cup heavy cream

2 Tbsp full-fat cream
  cheese

4 thyme sprigs,
  leaves stripped

½ Tbsp Dijon
  mustard

½ cup shredded
  extra-sharp
  cheddar

salt and black
  pepper

This dish is inspired by a certain kangaroo-inhabited country. However, when I initially made it, I got absolutely annihilated on social media for not doing it the "traditional" way. Well, I'm gonna just come out and say it... it may have been a bit different, but it was absolutely delicious. Oz, you've got better weather and exotic wildlife, and it's acceptable to walk around barefoot, so just let me have this.

─────

1. Fill a saucepan with cold water, add plenty of salt, then tip in the potatoes. Place the pan over a high heat and bring the water to a boil. Reduce the heat and leave on a gentle boil for 7–9 minutes, until the potatoes fall off the tip of a knife. Drain in a colander, cover with a clean dish towel and leave to steam-dry for 5 minutes.

2. Heat a frying pan over a medium heat. Add the bacon and fry for about 8 minutes, until the fat has rendered out and the bacon is crispy. Throw in the garlic and fry for 2 minutes, until fragrant. Leave to cool slightly.

3. In a large mixing bowl, whisk together the cream, cream cheese, thyme leaves and Dijon. Season well with salt and pepper. Chuck in the slightly cooled bacon, then add the sliced potatoes and stir through gently, so the potatoes don't break up.

4. Heat the oven to 400°F.

5. Pour the mixture into an ovenproof dish (see tip, page 206) and sprinkle over the cheddar. Put this in the oven for 30–40 minutes, until the cream mixture has reduced and the cheese is melted and golden.

Serves 6

CHRISTMAS DAUPHINOISE

1 cup heavy cream

1 garlic clove, peeled

pinch of white
  pepper

3 whole cloves

2 whole allspice
  berries

1 whole star anise

3–4-inch cinnamon
  stick

2¼ lbs Yukon Gold
  potatoes, peeled
  and sliced into
  ¼-inch rounds

7 oz brie, sliced

1 cup shredded
  extra-sharp
  cheddar

about 9 sage leaves

pinch of ground
  nutmeg

salt

Honestly – it's worth being on Santa's naughty list if it means I get to eat this Christmas dauphinoise every single day of December. This is my kinda advent calendar. And yeah, it's not the healthiest potato dish, but in the words of legendary fellow Brummie Noddy Holder, "It's CHRISTMASSSSS!" The big man himself would pick this over a cookie and glass of milk any day.

———

1. Heat your oven to 375°F.

2. Pour the cream into a saucepan and add the garlic, white pepper and whole spices. Place the pan over a medium heat and leave the cream to warm for 8–10 minutes, until thickened slightly. Remove the pan from the heat.

3. Remove the whole spices from the cream and add the potatoes to the pan – make sure you get all the spices out otherwise someone will be crunching down on that bark!

4. Tip the potato and cream mixture into an ovenproof dish (see tip, page 206, for how to choose the right size) and get them into an even layer.

5. Place the brie slices evenly over the top. Cover loosely with foil, then bake the potatoes for 30 minutes, until just tender. Scatter over the cheddar and the sage leaves, lower the oven to 350°F and bake for a further 20–30 minutes, until the cheese is golden and bubbling.

6. Serve up as a snack or the carby star of your dinner. But most importantly, dig in and Merry Christmas!

HASSELBACK BAKE

6 large Yukon Gold
  potatoes

olive oil

1⅔ cups heavy
  cream

2 Tbsp freshly grated
  parmesan

small bunch of
  chives, chopped,
  plus optional extra
  to serve

1 tsp smoked paprika

1 tsp garlic powder

1 tsp onion powder

5-6 oz extra-sharp
  cheddar, cut into
  ¼-inch-thick slices
  (or use cheddar
  cheese slices), plus
  an extra handful of
  shredded cheddar
  for topping

3 Tbsp butter, chilled
  and thinly sliced

salt and black
  pepper

In essence, this is a hasselback dauphinoise, which makes it instantly iconic in my opinion. All the creamy, rich goodness seeps into the hasselbacks, filling each slit while maintaining that CROUNCH. It's so naughty. I'm genuinely salivating and it is not attractive. I just love these so much.

———

1. Heat the oven to 375°F.

2. One potato at a time, lay the handles of two wooden spoons either side of the potato, then make vertical cuts all along the length so that you cut almost through, but the spoon handles stop you cutting through completely (a fully sliced, collapsed potato is definitely not what we're looking for). Chopsticks will do a good job of this, if you have them.

3. Place the potatoes snugly in a baking dish and drizzle with olive oil. Season with salt and pepper, then roast for 30 minutes, until the potatoes are just starting to brown.

4. Meanwhile, in a pitcher, mix together the cream, parmesan, chives, smoked paprika, garlic powder and onion powder with a pinch each of salt and pepper to season. Set aside for later.

5. When the potatoes have roasted, remove the dish from the oven. Turn the oven down to 325°F, and leave the potatoes until they are cool enough to handle. Breaking up the cheddar slices as you go, alternate cheddar and butter into the cuts in each hasselback and pour the cream and parmesan mixture around the potatoes in the baking dish – try not to get it over the top of the spuds or you won't have a crispy finish.

6. Sprinkle over the shredded cheddar and bake for 20–25 minutes, or until the potatoes are cooked through and the cheddar is golden brown. Top with a few extra chopped chives, if you fancy!

TOMATO FETA POTATO FAN

1 block of feta
(about 8 oz)

9 oz (about 1⅔ cups)
cherry or grape
tomatoes

3 garlic cloves,
peeled

1 tsp dried oregano

olive oil

small handful of basil
leaves

1¼ cups vegetable
broth

6–7 Yukon Gold
potatoes (or more,
depending on how
large your pan is),
peeled

2 Tbsp butter, cut
into small pieces

salt and black
pepper

A potato fan. Exactly what I am. If you're fancying going a bit extra-boujee with your potato bake next time, fan out your spuds. I never thought I'd be writing the words "fan out your spuds", but here we are. I think we need that on t-shirts.

——

1. Heat the oven to 425°F.

2. Place the block of feta in a round or oval ovenproof dish and put the tomatoes around the edge. Add the garlic cloves and sprinkle over the oregano. Then, drizzle over a little olive oil and season well with salt and pepper.

3. Roast the feta and tomatoes for 30 minutes, until everything is soft. Then, mash them together in the dish, add the basil leaves and vegetable broth and set aside. Keep the oven on.

4. While the feta is cooking, thinly slice the potatoes, trying to keep them in the order you slice them – you want to maintain each potato's shape, just in a sliced version, if you get me. It will save time when you start fanning and makes it all neater.

5. On top of your feta situation, start fanning out the slices of potatoes. They should almost stand up rather than lie flat. Continue adding potatoes until you've completely covered the dish.

6. Brush olive oil all over the potatoes, season well with salt and pepper and cover with foil. Bake for 50 minutes, then remove the foil, brush with more olive oil and top with the pieces of butter. Return the dish to the oven for a further 20–30 minutes, until the potatoes are golden and cooked through.

BOULANGÈRE POTATOES

Serves 6

7 Tbsp–½ cup plus
  2 Tbsp butter, plus
  extra if needed

2 onions, sliced

2¼ lbs russet
  potatoes, peeled
  and thinly sliced

2–4 cups chicken or
  vegetable broth

salt and black
  pepper

This is a very fancy but easy-to-make French potato bake. Even its name is giving me opulence. Honestly, though, it's posh but simple – layers of sliced potatoes cooked in decadent broth and onions, which add to all the flavors you want in a potato side dish. I could eat this one every day.

____

1. Heat the oven to 350°F.

2. Melt a pat of the butter in a large frying pan over a medium–high heat. Add the onions and fry for 4–5 minutes, until softened and slightly colored. Tip the onions on to a plate.

3. In the same frying pan, melt another pat of the butter and, in batches if necessary, add the sliced potatoes. Fry each batch for 5 minutes, turning occasionally, until some of the slices are lightly browned at the edges (you may need to add a little extra butter as you go).

4. Using a slotted spoon, transfer each batch to an ovenproof dish. Add a layer of onions and season with salt and pepper before adding the next layer of potatoes. Layer up with onions and seasoning, then keep going like this, finishing with a layer of potatoes.

5. Pour your broth over your potatoes so that the liquid just covers them (you may not need it all). Cover the dish with foil (don't let it touch the potatoes because it will stick), and place the dish in the oven. Bake the potatoes for 30 minutes, then remove the foil and continue baking for another 30–40 minutes, until the potatoes are soft through and browned on top.

Easy Potato Bakes

Serves 4–6

TOMATO + VODKA POTATO BAKE

olive oil

2 shallots, sliced

2 garlic cloves, finely chopped or grated

1 tsp crushed red pepper flakes

2 Tbsp tomato paste

3 Tbsp vodka

1 x 14-oz can of whole peeled tomatoes

⅔ cup heavy cream

2 lbs Yukon Gold potatoes, peeled

splash of chicken broth or water

5–6 cherry or grape tomatoes, halved

1 cup shredded mozzarella

salt and black pepper

few basil and rosemary leaves, to garnish

Vodka pasta went viral – it blew everyone's mind that a splash of the hard stuff in your pasta sauce could result in something glorious. So, I thought I'd swap out the pasta for some spuds, because why not? I find with most things in life, swap in a spud and you're on to a winner. Maybe not in a trifle.

———

1. Heat your oven to 350°F.

2. Heat a large frying pan over a medium heat. Add a splash of oil and the shallots and fry for 5–7 minutes, until light golden brown. Add the garlic and red pepper flakes and cook for another 2–3 minutes, until softened and fragrant.

3. Stir in the tomato paste and deglaze the pan with the vodka. Tip in the canned tomatoes and use a fork to smush them up. Add the cream, then leave the liquid to reduce for a few minutes while you slice your potatoes about ⅛ inch thick. Place the slices in a bowl of water while you finish the sauce.

4. Blitz your reduced sauce with a hand blender until thick and smooth, then taste for seasoning, adjusting with salt and pepper as necessary. Add the splash of broth or water if the sauce is very thick.

5. Begin layering your potato slices into a rectangular baking dish (about 11 x 7 inches, but see the tip on page 206 for how to find the right size), pouring over your sauce between each layer. Top with parchment paper and bake for 1½ hours, until the potatoes are cooked through.

6. Turn up the heat on the oven to 400°F and remove the dish of potatoes. Discard the parchment paper from the top, then dot over the halved tomatoes (cut side up) and sprinkle over the mozzarella. Finish with a garnish of basil and rosemary leaves and put the dish back into the oven for 10–15 minutes, until the top is golden brown and bubbling.

Easy Potato Bakes

Chapter
Nine

Extra
Crispies

CLASSIC CRISPY CUBES

2¼ lbs Yukon Gold potatoes, peeled and cut into ¾-inch cubes

¼ cup neutral oil, plus extra for the garlic

1 whole head of garlic

3 rosemary sprigs, 1 sprig left whole, 2 sprigs leaves picked and chopped

¼ cup freshly grated parmesan, plus optional extra to serve

salt and black pepper

These crispy cubes need to enter your life, marry you, have kids with you and live happily ever after... they're that perfect. This dish was my first proper viral video and cemented my status as "that random potato girl on TikTok". Ahh, good times.

————

1. Put the potatoes into a large saucepan of heavily salted, cold water. Place the pan over a high heat, bring the water to a boil, then reduce the heat and leave on a gentle boil for 5–7 minutes, until the potatoes fall off the tip of a knife. Drain in a colander. Leave the potatoes in the colander over the pan on the turned-off stove top, cover with a clean dish towel and leave to steam-dry for 10 minutes.

2. Meanwhile, heat your oven to 400°F. Add the oil to a rimmed baking sheet and place in the oven for the oil to get HOT. This is important for getting that crispy crunchiness.

3. Cut the top off the head of garlic and place it in some foil with the whole sprig of rosemary, a touch of oil and a sprinkle of salt. Then, wrap tightly.

4. Get the hot baking sheet out of the oven, then carefully tip in the potatoes and add the wrapped garlic. Roast the potatoes for 30 minutes, then remove the sheet, give the potatoes a mix and put them back in the oven for a further 15 minutes, until completely golden and crispy. Keep an eye on them in case you need less or more time.

5. Remove your potatoes and garlic from the oven and get the garlic and rosemary out of the foil. Squeeze the garlic flesh out of the cloves into a bowl and mix it with the chopped rosemary and the parmesan to form a paste.

6. Get all of that paste on to the potatoes, season with salt and pepper and give them a good toss. You're ready to serve, sprinkled with extra parmesan, if you wish. Remember: each bite should be super-CROUNCHY.

TIP: DEEP-FRYING YOUR CUBES

If you cba with waiting on the oven and you have a deep fryer, then, after steam-drying, you can instead fry these babies at 350°F in batches for about 2 minutes, until golden and crispy. Drain on paper towel, then dig in.

HONEY-GLAZED CRISPY CUBES + FETA

Serves 4

2¼ lbs Yukon Gold potatoes, peeled and cut into ¾-inch cubes

¼ cup neutral oil

1 whole head of garlic

3 slices of bacon, cut into pieces

2 Tbsp honey

pinch of crushed red pepper flakes

salt

about ⅓ cup crumbled feta, to serve

Italian parsley, leaves chopped, to garnish (optional)

finely chopped red chili, to garnish (optional)

Glazed, dazed and amazed – the words I'd use to sum up how I feel after devouring a family-sized portion of these babies. They've just got it all going on: that tangy hit of feta, the sweetness from the honey and the fluffy goodness of the spuds. Plus bacon. Perfection in a (supersized) bowl.

1. Get your potatoes into a saucepan of heavily salted, cold water. Place the pan over a high heat and bring the water to a boil. Reduce the heat and leave the potatoes on a gentle boil for 5–7 minutes, until they fall off the tip of a knife. Drain in a colander. Leave the potatoes in the colander to steam-dry with a dish towel over the top for 10–15 minutes.

2. Meanwhile, heat the oven to 400°F and get the oil into a rimmed baking sheet. Put the sheet into the oven to get the oil hot. This is important for getting that crispy crunchiness.

3. Cut the top off the head of garlic and place it in some foil with a touch of oil and a sprinkle of salt. Then, wrap tightly.

4. Get the hot baking sheet out of the oven, then carefully tip in the potatoes and add the wrapped garlic. Roast the potatoes for 30 minutes, then give them a mix and put them back in the oven for a further 15 minutes, until super-golden and crunchy all over. Keep an eye on them in case you need less or more time.

5. Place a frying pan over a medium–high heat. Add the bacon and fry for 5 minutes, until golden brown. Add the honey and red pepper flakes, then tip in the potatoes. Unwrap the garlic and squeeze in the soft, sweet cloves (use as many or as few as you like, to taste). Toss everything together.

6. Scatter over the crumbled feta, then serve garnished with the parsley and sprinkled with chopped chili, too, if you like.

Extra Crispies

CRISPY POTATO BALLS

Makes 24

1¾ lbs Yukon Gold potatoes

neutral oil

½ cup freshly grated parmesan

1 Tbsp cornstarch

sprinkle of store-bought crispy fried onions

handful of sage leaves, finely chopped, plus extra to serve

FOR THE DIP

3 Tbsp mayonnaise

3 Tbsp sour cream

1 garlic clove, crushed (smoked garlic is great for this)

small bunch of chives, finely chopped

salt and black pepper

After sampling these balls, you won't want anything else in your mouth. This is the perfect sharer that will elevate your classic "chips and dips" to the next level. You can make the balls up to three days in advance of frying. Just roll them up, cover them with plastic wrap and keep them in the fridge until you're ready.

——

1. Heat the oven to 425°F. Line a baking sheet with parchment paper.

2. Rub your potatoes with oil and a good amount of salt, and pierce them all over with a fork. Place them on a rack in the middle of the oven and bake for about 50–60 minutes, until tender on the inside and crisp on the outside. Remove from the oven and leave until cool enough to handle. Slice the potatoes in half and scoop out the flesh into a mixing bowl. Set this aside for later.

3. Make the dip. Stir together the mayo, sour cream, garlic and chives. Season well with salt and pepper, then transfer the dip to the fridge while you make the balls.

4. Mash the potato in the mixing bowl until smooth. Mix this with the parmesan, cornstarch, crispy onions and chopped sage. Season with plenty of salt and pepper.

5. Divide the mixture into 24 equal portions (about 1 Tbsp each), then, using your hands, shape each portion into a ball about the size of a ping-pong ball. Place the balls on the lined baking sheet as you go.

6. Pour your oil into a deep fryer or a heavy-based saucepan (don't let it come more than halfway up the inside of the pan). Place the pan over a high heat and get the oil to 350°F on a candy thermometer (or use the thermometer in your fryer). In small batches so as not to overfill the pan, add the balls and fry for 4 minutes, turning, until they are dark golden brown and crispy. Set each batch aside to drain on paper towel while you fry the remainder.

7. Pile up the balls on a plate, sprinkle with sage and serve warm with the dip.

CRISPY HOISIN DUCK POTATO CUBES

Serves 4

2 duck legs

1 heaping tsp Chinese five-spice powder

2 Tbsp hoisin sauce

1¾ lbs Yukon Gold potatoes

¼ English cucumber, sliced into thin strips

1 scallion, sliced into thin strips

salt

sesame seeds, to garnish (optional)

All the deliciousness of your local Chinese restaurant without the cost. I even threw in some cucumber and scallion strips to give you that added illusion of health. If you see green, it's basically a salad, right?

_____

1. Heat the oven to 400°F.

2. Dry the skin of the duck legs with paper towel and rub in the Chinese five spice and a pinch of salt. Place the legs in a roasting pan, skin side up, and roast for 1¼ hours, basting every 30 minutes with the rendered fat.

3. Glaze the roasted legs with some of the hoisin sauce (you won't need it all at this stage), brushing it over the skin, then return the legs to the oven for 15 minutes, until crispy and sticky.

4. Towards the end of the duck cooking time, peel, then chop your spuds into ¾-inch cubes. Get your potatoes into a saucepan of heavily salted, cold water. Place the pan over a high heat and bring the water to a boil. Reduce the heat and leave on a gentle boil for 5–7 minutes, until the potatoes fall off the tip of a knife. Drain in a colander. Place the colander over the pan on the turned-off stove top, cover with a clean dish towel and leave the potatoes to steam-dry for 10 minutes.

5. Once the duck is ready, pour a layer of the duck fat from the roasting pan into a separate rimmed baking sheet and carefully tip the steam-dried potato cubes into the hot fat. Stir gently to coat.

6. Roast the cubes for 30 minutes, then turn them over so they can color evenly and give them another 15 minutes, until crunchy and golden.

7. Meanwhile, shred the meat from the duck legs with two forks, discarding the bones, and toss the meat in the remaining hoisin to give it a good glaze. Keep warm.

8. Tip all of the crispy cubes into a serving dish and top with the shredded duck. Arrange the cucumber and scallions over the top. Finish with a sprinkling of sesame seeds, if you wish.

SALT + VINEGAR CRISPY CUBES

2¼ lbs Yukon Gold
potatoes, peeled
and cut into
¾-inch cubes

7 Tbsp malt vinegar,
plus extra to serve

¼ cup neutral oil

flaky sea salt,
to serve

I'm the sort of person who delves to the depths of the bag of fries for those crispy scraps bobbing about in a sea of vinegar, and this recipe is reminiscent of those flavors. These cubes are perfect served alongside battered cod, for a truly British experience, and some fluorescent curry sauce.

———

1. Get your potatoes into a saucepan of heavily salted, cold water. Add the vinegar, place the pan over a high heat and bring the liquid to a boil. Reduce the heat and leave on a gentle boil for 5–7 minutes, until the potatoes fall off the tip of a knife. Drain in a colander. Place the colander over the pan on the turned-off stove top, cover with a clean dish towel and leave the potatoes to steam-dry for 10 minutes.

2. Meanwhile, heat the oven to 400°F and get the oil into a rimmed baking sheet. Put the sheet into the oven to get the oil hot. This is important for getting that crispy crunchiness.

3. Once the potatoes have steam-dried, get the hot baking sheet out of the oven, carefully tip in the potatoes and turn to coat. Roast the potatoes for 30 minutes, then give them a mix and put them back in the oven for a further 15 minutes, until super-golden and crunchy. Keep an eye on them in case they need less or more time. (Alternatively, you can fry them in a fryer – see the tip on page 222.)

4. Serve sprinkled with flaky sea salt and an extra dousing of vinegar.

CAJUN-STYLE CRISPY CUBES

2¼ lbs Yukon Gold
  potatoes, peeled
  and cut into
  ¾-inch cubes

¼ cup neutral oil

FOR THE SAUCE

1 Tbsp butter

olive oil

1 onion, diced

1 green bell pepper,
  seeded and diced

2 garlic cloves, thinly
  sliced

1 tsp smoked paprika

½ tsp onion powder

½ tsp garlic powder

½ tsp dried oregano

½ tsp dried basil

½ tsp celery salt

pinch of crushed red
  pepper flakes

½ Tbsp tomato paste

1 large tomato, seeded
  and diced

⅔ cup chicken broth

1 Tbsp full-fat cream
  cheese

juice of 1 lime

salt and black pepper

I might've failed English Language school exam, but my alliteration is on point. My Cajun-style crispy cubes are inspired by my travels and packed full of flavor. The ingredient list may look extensive, but these are worth a raid of the spice cabinet.

____

1. Get your potatoes into a saucepan of heavily salted, cold water. Place the pan over a high heat and bring the water to a boil. Reduce the heat and leave on a gentle boil for 5–7 minutes, until the potatoes fall off the tip of a knife. Drain in a colander. Place the colander over the pan on the turned-off stove top, cover with a clean dish towel and leave the potatoes to steam-dry for 10 minutes.

2. Meanwhile, heat the oven to 400°F and get the neutral oil into a rimmed baking sheet. Put the sheet into the oven to get the oil hot. This is important for getting that crispy crunchiness.

3. Get the hot baking sheet out of the oven and carefully tip in the potatoes and turn to coat. Roast the potatoes for 30 minutes, then give them a mix and put them back in the oven for a further 15 minutes, until super-golden and crunchy. Keep an eye on them in case they need less or more time.

4. When the potatoes have about 20 minutes to go, make your sauce. Melt the butter with a splash of olive oil a large frying pan over a medium–high heat. Throw in the onion and fry for 7–8 minutes, until the onion is softened and golden. Add the green bell pepper and garlic and fry for 2–3 minutes, until fragrant.

5. Chuck in the paprika, onion and garlic powders, dried herbs, celery salt and red pepper flakes and season well with salt and pepper. Add the tomato paste and cook it for a few minutes, until it's all smelling delicious. Add the fresh tomato and pour in the chicken broth. Use a spatula to scrape up any bits of spices that have stuck to the bottom of the pan. Leave the sauce to bubble away for about 7–10 minutes over a medium heat, until reduced and thick.

6. Add the cream cheese, stir to combine and taste for seasoning. It should be the consistency of slightly thickened heavy cream.

7. Season the sauce with lime juice, and more salt and pepper, then serve up alongside the crunchy cubes of potato, with a little poured over the top to kick things off, if you like.

The Things You Can Achieve with the Humble Spud...

SMASHED POTATOES

Serves 4

1 lb 2 oz baby white
  potatoes

2 tsp sweet paprika

2 tsp ground cumin

1 tsp ground
  coriander

pinch of ground
  cinnamon

1 tsp crushed red
  pepper flakes

3 Tbsp olive oil

juice of ½ lemon

salt

Got any pent-up rage brewing? Whack out the spuds and give 'em a good bash. This is my therapy. After hearing "She needs to lay off the potatoes and pick up a salad" or "Get back to washing the pots" for the umpteenth time, a nice potato-smashing really sorts me out. Give it a go and release that anger, babs. x

———

1. Get your potatoes into a saucepan of heavily salted, cold water. Place the pan over a high heat and bring the water to a boil. Reduce the heat and leave on a gentle boil for 15–20 minutes, until the potatoes fall off the tip of a knife. Drain in a colander. Place the colander over the pan on the turned-off stove top and leave to steam-dry with a dish towel over the top for 10 minutes.

2. Meanwhile, heat the oven to 450°F.

3. Toast your spices in a dry pan over a medium heat until you can start smelling them (about 40 seconds). Don't let them burn – keep an eye on them. Remove the pan from the heat, then add your olive oil and lemon juice to the pan and season with salt.

4. Pour the spice mixture into the colander with the steam-dried potatoes and give the spuds a turn to coat them in all that lovely flavor. Tip them into a rimmed baking sheet and squash them slightly using the bottom of a jar or can, or punch them if you're feeling stressed (just let it out), so they have lots of edges to go crunchy. Bake for 40–45 minutes, giving the potatoes a toss halfway through cooking, until charred and crispy.

5. Once the potatoes are ready, put them in a suitable vessel and sprinkle with a bit more salt.

EXTRA-CRISPY SMASHED SPUDS

2¾ lbs Yukon Gold
potatoes, halved
(no need to peel)

1 tsp onion powder

1 tsp garlic powder

1 tsp smoked paprika

pinch of English
mustard powder
(optional)

pinch of fennel
seeds

pinch of ground
allspice

1 tsp salt

neutral oil

Nothing described as "extra-crispy" is ever bad. We all fight
over those crispy bits, so let's take away the fork dueling
and deliver a full bowl of crunchy goodness. Serve with your
favorite dip and make this your next movie-night snack.

——

1. Get your potatoes into a saucepan of heavily salted, cold water. Place the pan
   over a high heat and bring the water to a boil. Reduce the heat and leave on a
   gentle boil for 20–25 minutes, until the potatoes fall off the tip of a knife. Drain
   in a colander. Place the colander over the pan on the turned-off stove top and
   leave to steam-dry with a dish towel over the top for 5–10 minutes.

2. Meanwhile, heat your oven to 400°F.

3. Mix all your dry seasonings, herbs and spices together with the salt
   and set aside.

4. On a large rimmed baking sheet, space out the potatoes and use the bottom
   of a jar or can to press down and crush them so they have lots of edges to
   go crispy.

5. Sprinkle over the spice mixture and a drizzle of oil. Roast the potatoes for
   40 minutes, then flip them over and roast for 10–20 minutes more, until almost
   glass-like, shiny and crunchy.

CHIMICHURRI SMASHED POTATOES

Serves 4

2¼ lbs Yukon Gold
potatoes, halved
(no need to peel)

olive oil

salt and black
pepper

sour cream, to serve

**FOR THE
CHIMICHURRI**

7 Tbsp olive oil

2 Tbsp red wine
vinegar

large bunch of
Italian parsley,
leaves finely
chopped

large bunch of
cilantro, leaves
finely chopped

2 garlic cloves, finely
chopped

1 red chili, seeded
and finely chopped

¾ tsp dried oregano

1 tsp flaky sea salt

Usually reserved for grilled meat, chimichurri is today gracing our potatoes with its wonderfully fresh and vibrant sauciness. Marvel at the intense flavor and see this become your next signature dish – it's truly incredible at any BBQ or served alongside a big, fat juicy steak. Watch out potato salad, you might be usurped.

———

1. First, make the chimichurri. Mix all the chimichurri ingredients together in a bowl, then leave the sauce to sit while you make the potatoes (chimichurri gets better with time, so, if you can, make this the night before – or even a couple of hours before you need it – it will be amazing, as it will have released all the flavors).

2. Get your potatoes into a saucepan of heavily salted, cold water. Place the pan over a high heat and bring the water to a boil. Reduce the heat and leave on a gentle boil for 20–25 minutes, until the potatoes fall off the tip of a knife. Drain in a colander. Place the colander over the pan on the turned-off stove top and leave to steam-dry with a dish towel over the top for 5–10 minutes.

3. Meanwhile, heat your oven to 400°F.

4. On a large rimmed baking sheet, space out the potatoes and use the bottom of a jar or can to press down and crush them so they have lots of edges to go crispy. Drizzle with olive oil and season well with salt and pepper.

5. Roast the potatoes for 30–40 minutes, until crispy and golden, then flip them over. Spread over some of the chimichurri and return the baking sheet to the oven for 10–15 minutes, until you can smell that fragrant sauce and the spuds are crunchy to look at.

6. When the potatoes come out of the oven, serve with the remaining chimichurri (drizzled over the top is good, or in a saucy pool) and, of course, plenty of sour cream for dunking.

SMASHED POTATO NACHOS

Serves 4

2¾ lbs Yukon Gold
  potatoes, halved
  (no need to peel)

salt and black
  pepper

**FOR THE
SPICED OIL**

1 tsp smoked paprika

1 tsp garlic powder

2 Tbsp olive oil

**FOR THE PICKLED
RED ONION**

1 red onion, thinly
  sliced

juice of 3–4 limes

pinch of granulated
  sugar

**TO SERVE +
GARNISH**

1 ripe avocado

½ red onion,
  finely diced

juice of 1 lime

small bunch of
  cilantro, leaves
  finely chopped

3 slices of American
  processed cheese

splash of whole milk,
  or as needed

sour cream

sliced pickled
  jalapeños

sliced red chili

sliced scallions

A nacho dish... without the nachos. Hear me out, though. Sometimes I find with nachos that the toppings are insanely good, but then you dig a lil' deeper and are faced with those sad, bland tortilla crisps that no amount of cheese can save. I've rectified that. Say goodbye to the chips and hello to golden, crunchy, smashed potatoes.

———

1. Get your potatoes into a saucepan of heavily salted, cold water. Place the pan over a high heat and bring the water to a boil. Reduce the heat and leave on a gentle boil for 20–25 minutes, until the potatoes fall off the tip of a knife. Drain in a colander. Place the colander over the pan on the turned-off stove top and leave to steam-dry with a dish towel over the top for 5–10 minutes.

2. Meanwhile, heat your oven to 400°F.

3. On a large rimmed baking sheet, space out the potatoes and use the bottom of a jar or can to press them down and crush them so they have lots of edges to go crispy.

4. To make the spiced oil, mix together the smoked paprika, garlic powder and a big pinch each of salt and pepper with the olive oil. Use some of this to brush all over the potatoes, then roast them in the oven for 30–40 minutes, before flipping them over, brushing with a little more spiced oil, and roasting for 15–20 minutes more, until the spiced oil has turned a dark red and the potatoes are cooked and crispy.

5. Meanwhile, mix together the ingredients for the pickled red onion (you want just enough lime juice to cover them) and leave to soften and infuse for at least 10 minutes, then set aside.

6. Pit the avocado and scoop out the flesh into a bowl. Smash the avocado with a fork and mix through the diced red onion, lime juice and chopped cilantro. Season well with salt and pepper.

7. In a small microwaveable bowl, microwave the cheese slices with the splash of milk, on full power in 30-second bursts. Stir after each burst, until the cheese has melted to a sauce. Add in a bit more milk if it is a little thick.

8. Layer up the potatoes with the pickled onions, dollops of guacamole and sour cream, and a few jalapeño and chili slices, then drizzle with the cheese sauce and garnish with a sprinkling of scallions.

THE POTATO CAKE

olive oil

4 onions, thinly sliced

1 Tbsp dark brown sugar

1 tsp white wine vinegar

10 oz smoked bacon

4 large garlic cloves, thinly sliced

6¼ cups mashed potatoes (see page 16)

2 x 9-inch potato rösti (see page 136)

2 oz parmesan, plus extra to garnish

1 x 9-inch pommes Anna (see page 118)

2 x 6-inch potato rösti

1 x 6-inch pommes Anna

6–8 potato smiles (see page 74)

few chives, finely chopped

salt and black pepper

French fry candles, to garnish (optional)

BEFORE CONSTRUCTION

Heat the oven to 200°F and warm all the pre-made components.

Place your mashed potatoes in a microwaveable dish and warm it up in short bursts before piping.

I had to end the book with a showstopper, and here it is. At first, I called it the Potato Birthday Cake, but this beauty is too special to be limited to birthdays. Get it out for weddings, Christmas, Easter, christenings, bar mitzvahs, engagements, anniversaries – every event needs this potato cake. Layers of potato rösti, mashed potatoes, caramelized onion and bacon are topped with pommes Anna. I threw in a few potato smiles for good measure and French fry candles, too. Just cut the top off a candle and shove it in a fry. You'll need to triple the relevant recipe quantities of the rösti and pommes Anna to get what you need.

—

1. In a large frying pan over a medium heat, add a glug of olive oil and throw in your sliced onions. Lower the heat and cook them gently for about 20 minutes, until they turn a light golden brown. Season well with salt and pepper, then add in the brown sugar and white wine vinegar to deglaze the pan. Leave your onions to bubble away for 15–20 minutes over a low heat, until sticky and jammy. Set aside.

2. Heat your oven to 400°F. Put your bacon in a single layer in a rimmed baking sheet and bake for 10–15 minutes, until crispy. Chop the bacon into fine pieces, like a crumble, and set aside.

3. Pour about 1 inch of oil into the bottom of a small saucepan and place the pan over a medium–high heat. Add the garlic slices and leave to cook, turning occasionally for 2–4 minutes, until golden brown. Scoop out the garlic and drain it on paper towel. Set aside.

4. Now you can start to construct your cake. First, spoon about 10 tablespoons of the mash into a medium piping bag fitted with a medium open star tip. Set this aside. Place one of the 9-inch rösti on a serving plate. Spread with some of the remaining mashed potatoes (you are going to want 4 layers from this – two larger and two smaller – so divide it up appropriately) and top with caramelized onions and a sprinkle of bacon bits. Grate over some of the parmesan and top with the second 9-inch rösti. Repeat the toppings, then top the stack with the 9-inch pommes Anna.

5. Add a 6-inch rösti, repeat the toppings (mash, onions, bacon, parmesan), then add the second 6-inch rösti. Repeat the toppings again and finish with the final, smaller pommes Anna. From the filled piping bag, pipe swirls of mashed potatoes in a ring around the top edge. Position your potato smiles around the sides of the cake.

6. Finally, decorate the piped mashed potatoes with slices of the garlic and a final sprinkling of crispy bacon bits. Scatter over the chopped chives and give a final grating of parmesan. Add the fries with candles hidden inside, if you want to get everyone singing – just don't eat the fries afterwards. Amazing.

COOK'S NOTES

When it comes to making these dishes, I've cooked A LOT of potatoes to make sure you can replicate them at home to match. I have tried and tested with different potato variations, sizes from different stores, and more – and one thing has become clear: potatoes are an unreliable beast and some harvests just ain't great. Sometimes the sugar content can be too high, sometimes the starch is too starchy – these and other variables can mean that your roasted potatoes are different from one week to the next. So, in general, I suggest buying the best-quality spuds you can and take my advice on the type of potato where you can.

THE SIZE OF YOUR POTATOES

I've based all the mashed potatoes recipes on serving two people. In this case, my rule of thumb is one potato per person and a little extra. On average, the weight of one potato used in the recipes is about 7 oz.

For roasted potatoes, I've suggested quartering them before you boil – in which case, you need to make sure you have potatoes that are at least medium sized (again, about 7 oz per potato). This will give you even-sized quarters to work with. If your potatoes are smaller, just think to yourself, "Could I eat this whole potato in one mouthful?" If that's a yes, then just peel and boil; if it's a "no", but the potato is still on the small size, then cut it in two. If it's a "Hell, no!", quarter it.

SIDES AND MAINS

Most dishes in the book are intended for serving alongside something else – which I've mostly left to your imagination (plus to give all those suggestions would have made this book longggg and less about the potatoes). If you need further inspiration, check out my socials; or if you're like me, just see what's on sale at the supermarkets and go from there. The potatoes will be the star anyway – they're always the best bit.

FRYING

Let's talk deep fryers – I've used them a lot in this book and, frankly, they go hand in hand with potatoes. I just want you to be careful with them. Never take your eyes off the fryer and keep any unnecessary liquids away from them. Also make sure no children or vulnerable people are left alone with a fryer. As soon as you are done with the frying part, turn it off. Unplug it to be certain.

An alternative to a fryer is to use a deep saucepan of oil on the stove top. If you do this, then please make sure you fill the pan only halfway. This means that there's space for the potatoes to cook and not bubble over. Apparently, after Heston Blumenthal started the whole triple-cooked-fries craze, the number of accidental house fires in the UK went up. So please use with caution; I know they say any publicity is good publicity but I don't want a fire on my conscience. Move the pan from the stove altogether once you've finished frying and turn off the burner.

For both pan-frying and deep-frying, once the oil has cooled down, you can pour it back into its bottle and reuse it twice more. When it comes to getting rid of it, remember to put it in the trash in its bottle, completely cooled. Don't pour it down the drain!

If you are shallow-frying instead of deep-frying, use the same deep pan you would to deep-fry, but fill with enough oil to just cover your potatoes. This will take longer than deep-frying, but you'll use less oil overall.

I've mostly suggested using neutral oil – by which I mean peanut, vegetable or canola, say. Neutral oil won't impart flavor to your spuds. If a recipe specifies a particular type of oil, fat or butter that's because it's all part of the deliciousness.

GENERAL

All the eggs, veg and so on used in the recipes are medium unless specified otherwise. Likewise, use fresh herbs, unless I've specified dried.

That's it. You're good to go.

INDEX

THANK YOU

I have to start this off by thanking the most important thing in my life. You have been with me through thick and thin. You have taught me right from wrong. You have been with me on my best of days and cheered me up on the worst of days. You have pushed me to achieve so much. My rock. My life. My love. My everything. Thank you to the reason I am here... the Potato.

No, but seriously, beyond the spuds, I've been lucky enough to have an incredible team around me to make this book a reality. I am sorry for the number of potatoes you've all had to eat, read about, write about and eat again. It's all been worth it for this beauty of a book!

Big thanks to my team at Poppy Cooks, who have saved my life many-a-time during the writing. Kat – you (s)mashed it, helping to develop a lot of these recipes and I'm sorry for the amount of potato recipes you've had to test again and again over the last few months. It sounds like a dream job, but I think she'd be happy never seeing a potato again. Sam – thank you for trying to organize the most disorganized person in the world (me) and making sure everything (just about) was delivered on time. Holly – thank you for your help putting my thoughts and ramblings into writing and making sure the intros aren't too random with me talking absolute rubbish. Thank you to the wider team: Gary and Haz for your help keeping everything Poppy Cooks running in the background.

Thank you to the incredible book-shoot team, who made it an absolute dream pulling this book together. Our photographer Ellis Parrinder absolutely nailed the Poppy point of view and I love every single picture so much. I want them all as prints covering my house. On props was Max Robinson, who beautifully set up some incredible imagery in this book – I'm glad we got the pink latex in. Thank you to the absolute hero that is Valerie Berry, who headed up food styling on the day with help from Eden Owen Jones. These people deserve medals for the amount of potatoes they've had to endure over the last month.

Thank you once again to the dream team at Bloomsbury for working tirelessly to get this book together. Thank you to Rowan for heading up the project and believing in all things Poppy and Potatoes. To Emily and Kiron for keeping the train on the tracks for the last year and sorry I was late once or twice with a few bits... hehe! And to Emma for making the pages look beautiful. Thanks to Jude – the icon, the editor, the hero. You somehow got a girl who got Ds in her A-Levels and once said "Qu*m" on Live TV through her fourth book and that in itself deserves all the praise. Thank you to the PR & Marketing team of Ellen, Shunayna and Isobel for your incredible work to make sure people know about this book.

And finally thank you to my family for always being there, even when it's to distract me from the impending doom of having to write 100 potato recipes in a couple of months. Thank you to my parents Vicky and Jim for having to eat A LOT of leftover potatoes. Thank you to my 17-year-old brother Christian, who despite being obsessed with the gym, still always made room for a cheat carb or two. Thank you to my 14-year-old sister Trixie, who can say she actually came up with the cauliflower cheese potato skin recipe. I owe you. Thanks to my dogs, Krypto the pug and Red the German shepherd, for distracting me way too much and being too good at snuggling. And thank you to my fiancé Tom, who is the second love of my life – behind potatoes.

ABOUT POPPY

TV presenter, author, Michelin-trained chef and self-crowned Potato Queen, Poppy Cooks worked in professional kitchens for over a decade. Poppy rose to fame on TikTok and is now an internet sensation with over 4.3 million followers on the platform, and more than 1 million followers on Instagram.

This is Poppy's fourth book – she is already the author of three best-sellers. She is also the co-host of BBC Three's *Young MasterChef*, which launched its second series in January 2024, has been a judge on E4's *Celebrity Cooking School* and is a chef-mentor on ITV's *Cooking with the Stars*. Find Poppy @poppycooks on TikTok and @poppy_cooks on Instagram.

Appetite by Random House® and colophon are
registered trademarks of Penguin Random House LLC.

Library and Archives Canada Cataloguing in Publication
is available upon request.

ISBN: 978-0-525-61296-4
eBook ISBN: 978-0-525-61297-1

Photographer: Ellis Parrinder
Designer: Emma Wells, Studio Nic+Lou
Recipe Development: Poppy O'Toole and Kat Cooper
Food Stylists: Poppy O'Toole and Valerie Berry
Prop Stylist: Max Robinson

Printed in Canada

The authorized representative in the EU for product
safety and compliance is Penguin Random House
Ireland, Morrison Chambers, 32 Nassau Street, Dublin
D02 YH68, Ireland, https://eu-contact.penguin.ie

Published in Canada by Appetite by Random House®,
a division of Penguin Random House Canada Limited.
320 Front Street West, Suite 1400
Toronto, Ontario, M5V 3B6, Canada
penguinrandomhouse.ca

10 9 8 7 6 5 4 3 2